HOME
IS WHERE

HOME
IS WHERE
The Journeys of a Missionary Child

MARGARET
NEWBIGIN BEETHAM

DARTON · LONGMAN + TODD

First published in 2019 by
Darton, Longman and Todd Ltd
1 Spencer Court
140 – 142 Wandsworth High Street
London SW18 4JJ

ISBN: 978-0-232-53408-5

The publisher has been unable to trace copyright holders for the photographs on pp. 4 and
5 of the picture section. If anyone is able to provide evidence of copyright ownership we
would be very happy to provide full acknowledgment in future editions of the book.

A catalogue record for this book is available from the British Library

Designed and produced by Judy Linard
Printed and bound in Great Britain by Bell & Bain, Glasgow

For my Sister
Alison Christine Newbigin
1941–2005

'Love is strong as death.'

CONTENTS

PREFACE

My sister, Alison Christine Newbigin, died in March 2005 after a short illness. During her last few weeks we spent many hours together in the hospital and then in the hospice to which she moved and where she died. In the succeeding months I thought a good deal about the life we had shared as children, about remembering and forgetting, and what gets told and what does not. Our childhood experience was far removed from that of my own children and grandchildren. The airplane, the mobile phone and the internet have transformed the ways we keep in touch with family and friends from whom we are geographically separated, which makes the experience Ali and I shared with our younger sister, Janet, and brother, John, seem extraordinarily distant. However, there were other and more profound reasons than distance in time for why I had not thought of or spoken about those early years. Gradually, I began to confront my own 'forgetting', writing short pieces in which I recalled and tried to make sense of my memories. This book is the result.

My given names are Margaret Rachel and writing this memoir as 'Rachel' and using the third person, as I do here after the opening section, may seem, at best, contrary. However, it gave me permission to make up dialogue or even invent the content of letters and emails, though I always did this in order to be faithful to my memories and to existing evidence. Ironically, I found that writing in the third person released me to be more truthful. Perhaps it broke the barriers to memory and retelling which I had built up over a lifetime.

I hope, too, that using the third person will also point beyond my individual story to wider histories. Whatever the differences between my experience and that of my children, my early life shared much with that of my mother, born to missionary parents in 1907, or even to that of the two generations before hers going back to the earliest days of British missionaries being allowed to marry. Like those earlier generations, my parents were caught in the tensions between a commitment to love all equally as God's children and their entanglement in, and resistance to, colonial practices, including those of child-rearing. Living, as I do today, in a multi-cultural city and enjoying friendships with those from many parts of the world, I am painfully aware of the often-traumatic loss of home endured by those who become migrants, refugees or asylum seekers in our post-colonial world.

However, this is, of course, an account of a particular life. My parents, Lesslie and Helen Newbigin, brought their unique gifts to their lives as missionaries and to being our Dad and Mum. My father's Presbyterian inheritance did not include the practice of calling the priest 'Father' but I came to understand that many people wanted him to father them in some way, either as authority figure or nurturing parent. However, through it all he was still our Dad and that is how I have tried to write of him here. It is my account, told from a particular point of view, with my insights and blindness.

I have throughout used some of the words which were common in the speech of the British in India from the mid-nineteenth century onwards and have provided a brief glossary for those which may not be familiar to readers. This presents some problems of which the most acute is the familiar use of a word now so offensive that I have hesitated to write it. The uniform of the school to which I and my sisters were sent was described in all the School literature as 'nigger-brown'. This term was used with no sense of its racist nature by generations of missionaries and their children who attended the school. I have decided to use it on its first introduction and thereafter to omit it, but I do so reluctantly since this is a history where inevitably what we can celebrate and what we must condemn are utterly entangled.

My heart-felt thanks go to friends and family who supported me through the many years of this book's gestation. I am grateful to my sister, Jan Williamson, and brother, John Newbigin, who have read and commented on the typescript, as have my daughters, Helen and Kate Beetham, and my friend, Janet Batsleer. My thanks to all of them for their continuing support and love. Thanks, also, to my friend Miriam Hirst, who read and commented on some parts of my draft, as did my old school friends, Ruth Seal (née Porritt)

PREFACE

and Margaret Houston (née Moore), who sadly died in 2017. The members of my Writing Group in its various manifestations, have given wonderfully perceptive and productive criticism to earlier versions; thanks to Brenda Cooper, Viv Gardner, Ursula Hurley, Judy Kendall, Myna Trustram and Janet Wolff. Thanks, too, to David Moloney at Darton, Longman and Todd.

A note on names: I have changed the names of my immediate family and of my friends.

PERMISSIONS

A version of the chapters 'Dust' and 'Mango Season' were originally published as one chapter in *Writing Otherwise: experiments in cultural criticism* edited by Jackie Stacey and Janet Wolff (Manchester: Manchester University Press, 2013).

In the chapter 'Mango Season' the 'quotations' from websites are my own pastiches of similar websites. I have, however, drawn directly and indirectly on Dane Kennedy's *The Magic Mountains: Hill Stations and the British Raj* (Berkeley and Los Angeles: University of California Press, 1996) and I am grateful to him for his generous permission to do so.

I am grateful to the estate of Walter de la Mare for permission to quote from the poem, 'The Listeners' in the chapter 'The Invisible Thread'.

Thanks to the Estate of T. S. Eliot for permission to quote from his *Collected Poems, 1909–1962* (London, Faber and Faber) in the chapter *A Cold Coming…*

I

FIRST THINGS
(2016)

DRY BONES

I woke in the dark, hearing, through the double glazing, a blackbird singing in the street. The faint glow from the radio alarm showed the time as 6.00, but it felt like 5.00. The clocks had just gone forward. The earth tilting towards spring. I put on the bedside light which glinted off the framed photos on the bookcase by the bed. I love getting photos of my grandchildren on the phone but I still like an old-fashioned photo you can put in a frame. And of course, most of these were taken before digital was invented. There are my family on my parents' golden wedding anniversary; my mother, bird-like in her red dress, head slightly poked forward, my father smiling but not quite at whoever was taking the photo as, of course, he was almost blind by then. We are all smiling cheesily at the camera, except for Alison who is looking down, frowning a little. She didn't like family photos. Next to that I have put my favourite picture of her, Ali, my sister. She is sitting on her old sofa, just looking up from reading the paper, smiling, with her cat on her knee. Sparky the cat was called. I secretly called him Narky, because he always bit and scratched me, but she loved him.

When she was in the hospice and very near the end her neighbour, Jeff, smuggled the cat into her room in a cardboard box. When the box was opened the cat shot under the bed and would not come out. The nurses pretended they hadn't seen anything. At last Jeff managed to lift Sparky onto the bed where she could just touch his fur with her fingers. It was St David's Day. I know because Ali told me. Each day counted.

That morning one of the nurses had suggested a walk in the hospice garden. We had bundled her up in blankets – or rather the nurses did. I was useless, but I did find that woolly hat knitted by one of her friends, the one who kept crying and wanting Ali to make it all better for everyone else that she was dying. I told Ali it looked as if she was wearing a red and yellow tea cosy but at least it kept her head warm. The wheelchair was hard to push but we went slowly round the garden, not speaking much but looking in the slanting March sunlight. 'Look your last on all things lovely,' I thought but I just kept pushing and stopping to look with her. We looked at the snowdrops, the buds on the trees, the pond with its wind sculpture turning, the green spears of daffodils with the yellow hidden in them ready to burst out and trumpet the spring she would not live to see.

If this was India now I might drape the photos in garlands, honour the dead with flowers, but that seems extravagant and – after all – this is not India. This is Manchester and it is nearly the end of March. I am glad. The first three months of the year are too full now of the anniversaries of the dead. My father, my mother, my sister, my forty-year marriage. I wake now on my own. But they are there smiling in their frames, my dead and living family, my long loves.

This won't do, I thought, and got up to make myself a cup of tea.

'Who's that?' my friend Mary asked me the other day, peering at a rather faded photo I had hung at the bottom of the stairs.

'It's my Mum. I think it was the year she left school.'

'Where's your Dad, then?'

I realised then with something of a shock that I had not put up anywhere in the house a photo of my father on his own. The ones in my bedroom were always of him with my mother or family groups. In these he was always in mufti, never wearing a dog collar or a cassock. But, of course, like so many of my other dodges for trying to avoid the truth of the past, that strategy doesn't work. In the wooden box carved with elephants and palm trees which I inherited from my mother, I keep her collection of photos, some in albums, mostly stuck into folders and brown envelopes where I have tried to sort them. There are very few of us in our childhood. No easy access to film then and no sense that every moment must be recorded. But there are plenty of photos of my father, almost all showing him in some official capacity: wearing a white cassock as he visits an Indian village, caught in conversation at some World Council of Churches meeting with a group of other dog collars, greeting some visiting dignitary I vaguely recognise but can't quite put a name to.

He was well-known in our world was my Dad, Lesslie Newbigin, well-known in the world of church and especially in missionary circles. He has an after-life as a theologian, quoted in American blogs, copies of his books still sell. I am reminded of this regularly as the royalty cheques come in. I find myself now managing his literary estate. I am his 'executor', one of those legal words which carries a whiff of something terminal; execution, exit. I get fewer emails now from people asking me personal questions about my father, hungry for details and reminiscences.

Perhaps, I thought, I should get out one of those photos of my Dad and hang it in the hall too. But I did not go to the box of photos. Instead I made myself a cup of tea and drank it, standing and looking out of the kitchen window. The sky was brightening. A white moon – almost full – hung over the rooftops and chimneys pots. The tree in next door's garden was coming into blossom, the dark mesh of branches still showing through the opening buds. Soon it will be a white cloud suspended there. When the people who now live in that house bought it and began tidying the neglected garden, I went and asked them not to cut that tree down without talking to the neighbours. And now each spring and always taking me by surprise, the miracle of the blossom transforms my small garden, just as Cinderella was transformed in that version of the story I read as a child where it is standing under the magic tree which changes her from a kitchen skivvy into a princess.

I stood now cradling my mug of tea and looking out through my reflection at my back garden and the houses beyond. The sky was losing its bruised look. The blackbird started up again, insisting that it was spring and the world was new and beautiful but in my head going round and round was that negro spiritual 'Dem bones, dem bones dem – uh – dry bones, hear the word of the Lord' that we used to sing with my Dad at the piano. 'Play the bones song', we'd say. 'Play the bones song, please, please, Daddy.' And he would turn the flimsy pages and sing along while he played and we children danced around, 'And the foot bone connected to the – uh – ankle bone. And the ankle bone connected to the – uh – shin bone. Hear the word of the Lord.'

He called it 'the compensation piano'. 'Comp-en-say-shun.' It was a hard word to get your tongue round as a child. 'I bought it with the money I eventually got from the railway', Dad would explain to some visitor (there were always visitors). 'You know, just after I arrived in India I was involved in an accident on a bus at a level crossing. My foot was crushed. They said I would never walk again. I'm a miracle of modern medicine.' He would laugh. 'It was a miracle I got any money out of the railway, that's for sure.' He would close the piano, give us a quick kiss and stride off.

My father walked more quickly than anyone else I knew and he continued to do so into old age. Even when he was eighty and almost blind he would walk briskly up the escalators in the London Underground or march out into the middle of some busy street holding out his white stick while cars braked around him, their drivers cursing and pressing their horns. My memories of childhood walks up in the hills at Kodai were of half-walking, half-running along after him, sometimes looking back to make sure Alison was still there. I always knew I had to look after her. I couldn't remember the world without her, whereas I could remember the time before my younger sister and brother were born. Ali was close to me in age, but I was always the big sister. 'Keep up', I would say. 'Keep up!' Perhaps I have spent my life trying to keep up with my father. And why did I at some point let go of my sister's hand, fail to turn my head to see that she was not there?

The sky was brightening. 'I'll walk down to the river,' I thought. I got dressed quickly, humming to myself as I put on my boots, 'and the foot bone connected to the ...'. One advantage of living on my own – I don't have to consult anyone else or tell them I am going for an early morning walk. In the hall, I glanced at the photo of my Mum, a young woman in a gym slip, smiling and looking ready to spring up and keep up with anyone.

I let myself out of the house. In the street a few lights were coming on in upstairs rooms. The taxi driver at number 115 came out as I passed and got into his black cab. As I went into the Park I looked up at the huge ash tree which stands at the gates. Unlike the smooth grey of the younger ash which line the path beyond, this tree trunk is gnarled with age. Its branches stretch huge into the sky. Ever since I read about ash die-back I have decided to check this tree once a week for signs of die-back, though how to tell in winter I don't know. It looks dead now but I love the great rough trunk, the way the twigs all point upward at their tips, the black buds still tight. My neighbour, who always takes his dog to the park before work, greeted me. 'Lovely morning!' And it was.

The Mersey runs in its deep channel on the other side of the playing fields and through the scrubby woodland of the Country Park. I used to be able to get there in twenty minutes if I walked fast. I am still my father's daughter but now age has slowed my pace. This morning the river had sunk down from the level it was at a few days ago, leaving its detritus of branches and plastic rubbish. The Mersey here rises and falls rapidly. Before this high bank was built in the 1960s it regularly flooded all the fields around, which is why there is this belt of golf courses, playing fields, woods and rough terrain where I now love to walk. As I turned along the path above the high watermark I could see the Peak District, the source of the river, above the line of trees. The motor way roared past, invisible beyond the line of Manchester poplars on the other bank. A couple of ducks swept happily downstream. No heron today. The blackthorn hung its white blossom on bushes, here and there was green on the hawthorn twigs, but otherwise there were few signs of spring. Broken twigs and dry leaves lay on the path. Dry bones.

Hard to believe this is the same river we crossed once on the ferry with Auntie May on one of our school holidays. That was more than sixty years ago. She was taking us, Ali and me, to New Brighton as a treat but the real treat was going on the ferry from Liverpool across the Mersey, which was so wide there it was almost the sea. Of course, it wasn't the same Mersey all those years ago any more than I am the same me, but then, of course, it is and I am.

I turned away from the river down some wooden steps set in the bank so that I could cut back through the wood and cross the Chorlton Brook on the little foot bridge. In summer the balsam reaches up almost to the bridge and the stream is sluggish but now the banks were scraped clean by winter floods. Much of the brook is culverted and in the past was stained by industrial waste but now it runs clear and strong. The ancient apple tree on the far bank is the outpost of what was planted many years ago as a community orchard. In the autumn passers-by still pick up the apples to take home, though they are misshapen and too bitter to eat raw.

Easter is early this year and it will soon be here. Across the world in different languages churchgoers will hear that reading from Ezekiel, the story of the prophet who is taken to the valley of dry bones and told to prophesy to them. Can these bones live? And the foot bone connected to the – uh – ankle bone.

I walked more quickly back across the playing fields seeing several other walkers now, though I was the only one without a dog. Perhaps, I thought, I will get out a photo of my father. The past is not just a bag of old bones. I felt the wind on my cheek.

HANNAH

'Heavy things underneath. That's the rule.'

'What are you talking about?'

'My Mum's first commandment of packing,' I said. 'You know, helpful tips for how to get all you need for three weeks in Canada into a small case. My Mum was a brilliant packer.'

I was visiting my friend Hannah. She and I have been friends for so long that we can sit comfortably in silence for a few moments as we did now, me with my shoes off and my legs stretched out on her settee, she in the large armchair stroking the cat on her knee. Spring sunshine lit up the walls of her room with its collection of prints and family photos. I thought of my morning walk by the river, of the photos in Mum's old box.

'When's your flight?'

'A week tomorrow,' said Hannah. 'Can't quite believe it. I still can't believe Mum won't be there, even though it's ages since she died.'

'No. I can't believe it is so long since my Mum died.'

'You know,' Hannah went on, 'now I have grandchildren, I feel so regretful that I left Canada to live in England and deprived my Mum of the chance to see her grandson growing up as I do mine.'

'Yes. All those migrations. All those separations. My Mum wasn't around for most of my growing up. She did see our kids a bit but ...'. We drank our tea for a moment or two without speaking. 'It's no wonder my Mum was so good at packing,' I said.

'I don't think my parents brought much from the shtetl when they left Russia and once they got to Montreal they stayed all their lives,' Hannah said. 'Of course, my Mum's mother came with them so she was around for all our growing up. You know she only ever spoke Yiddish. I never heard her speak English.'

'I get such a shock when I look in the mirror now.'

'Tell me about it.'

'No, but I am looking more and more like my Mum.'

'Women turn into their mothers, which is their tragedy. Who said that?'

'"And men don't, which is theirs." Oscar Wilde, my dear, the blessed Oscar. Do you remember how in our women's group we were so determined that we would never be like our mothers?'

'Oh yes.' We both laughed and were silent for a moment thinking of the group in the 1970s where we first met, the passionate discussions, the feeling that anything was possible.

'Do you realize that was more than forty years ago?' I said. 'Of course, we didn't think then that we would ever be old.'

'No. And look at us now.' We laughed again and drank our coffee. 'But, you know, our lives have been different from our mothers. Look at you. Didn't you tell me your mother never worked after she got married?'

'No. She never earned her own money or drove a car or ... Her whole life was bound up with my Dad's. Dear Mum. But ...' I thought for a moment. 'But, you know, for the first – what? –seventeen years or so – my life followed hers very closely: India, missionary parents, sent back to the very same boarding school in England ...'

'You went to the same school as your Mum?'

'Yes, founded in 1838 "for the daughters of missionaries". I don't think much had changed there – even the colour of the uniform, which was officially "nigger brown". '

'What!'

I know. That is such an offensive word now but we all used it without any sense of its racism. But at the time ...'

'Of course. And even then. But, why did you never tell me about all that? About school and India and ... After all we have been friends for...' Her voice trailed off.

'I have been wondering that. Why was it so hard, so impossible, to talk about? I never let on about my parents or being brought up in India. It was like ... a shameful secret. Perhaps it was because in our circles any kind of faith was a no-no. And, perhaps it was a rebellion against, you know, the way missionaries were forever telling other people about their lives, what they were doing, sending news back home. It was part of their job.'

'Was it? Never met a missionary – except of course those people who come to the door sometimes.'

'Oh yes! All those missionary magazines and sermons and stories about good works in distant lands and – missionaries had to go on deputation when they came back home.'

'Deputation? Sounds painful.'

'Perhaps it was sometimes. It meant going round to different churches to tell them about your good works and, I suppose, make sure the money for missions kept coming in. I never thought about it as a child. It was just what Dad did when we were "home".'

'Home?'

'Back in Britain. And Mum and Dad always did one of those awful Christmas circular letters. I hated them.'

'Well I suppose it was a way of keeping in touch with a lot of people. No Facebook then.'

'You're right! It was a bit like Facebook. I hadn't thought of that. A cleaned-up version of our lives – you know – all those wonderful things we're doing …'

'Okay. Okay. Have a Grumpy Old Woman rant about Facebook. Didn't you tell me your Dad published his autobiography?'

'Yes, he did.'

'What about your Mum?'

'No way. I wish now I had asked her more about her life. But, you know she spent her life writing letters. Because she was always living away from her family and friends, usually in a different continent, and there were no phones or email or anything, she wrote letters, must have written thousands of them. So, in one way, she was always writing her life.'

'But not for publication. They were private, all those letters.'

'That's right. Not for publication.' We were silent again for a moment.

'You know when I was six or so I wanted to be called Rachel,' I said at last,

'Why Rachel?'

'It's my second name and I – don't know – perhaps I liked it more than Margaret. Every now and then I tried to make everyone call me Rachel, but it didn't work and, of course, at school I became 'Margaret'. You know if/when I write the story of my childhood I will write it as 'Rachel', that little girl who is me and not me.'

'Good Jewish name, Rachel.'

'Of course. Mum and Dad knew their Bible! But Mum told me I was called after her Irish aunties.'

'Irish?'

'Yes, that's another part of the story. My Mum's family were Irish. I thought you knew.'

'No. I didn't. So how come your Mum was brought up in India and then went to school in England?'

'I will tell you the whole tale sometime, but I must go.' I sat up and began to put on my shoes. 'Do you remember, Hannah, when we were talking a year or so after my Mum died and you suggested that I write a letter to her?'

'I wrote a letter to my Dad a few years after he died. There was so much I wanted to say to him.' We were silent again for a moment.

'I am glad you came from Canada or I wouldn't have known you,' I said at last. 'But it is great that you are going back for this visit.'

'Do you think you will go back to India again sometime?'

'Don't think so. I don't know. I must get going. Wish you still lived in Manchester.'

'Well it's only twenty miles or something.'

'Yes, but ...' I looked around again at the familiar room. 'Hannah, you are the only person I know who can get away with painting your walls pink. Are you trying to reclaim the dreaded P word?'

'Well, it is not exactly pink. But it does work, doesn't it? I think I get my colour sense from my father. You know eventually he became a buyer for the textile company he worked for. When he wasn't working for the overthrow of capitalism, he was obviously very good at his job.' She pushed the cat off her knee and stood up. 'You know, it's no wonder we get on so well. Me with my communist parents, you with your Christian missionaries. We were both brought up to think that the world could be saved and we had to do it.'

'I gave up on that one a while ago,' I said.

'Have you?' She was sceptical.

'My sister, Ali, you know, she had a postcard stuck up on one of her kitchen cupboards. It said *You don't have to save the world. That's my job, love God.*'

'Hmm,' said Hannah as I gave her a hug. 'Let's not go there now.'

As I drove back into Manchester I thought about those years in India, the time in boarding school; my memories of them were vivid but broken, islands sticking up above the sea of forgetting. Sometimes it felt as if I had been a different person then. Rachel, perhaps. I still have the Bible Dad gave me with both my names written in the front in his spidery writing, 'Margaret Rachel Newbigin', and a reference to Psalm 121, verse 8, 'The Lord will keep your going out and your coming in from this time forth for evermore'. Going out and coming in, they did a lot of that, Mum and Dad.

Perhaps I could write a letter to Mum but what was it I wanted to say? 'Dear Mum, you have been dead for so long but I have been thinking about you recently'? Or 'Dear Mum, Sorry I was so bad at saying "thank you" or "I do love you".' Really, it's not my kind of thing. It was more an Ali thing, writing letters to the dead. Hadn't she done something like that when we scattered Mum and Dad's ashes? She'd written on a piece of paper which she had torn up and scattered on the moor along with the grey powdery ash. It all went into the heather and grey, grey stones. Being Ali, she hadn't explained. I can't do that, I thought. I really can't. Bad enough turning into your mother. Much worse to turn into your younger sister.

'Oh, Ali!' My heart turned over, as it does so often now when I think of her, my sister, the one closest to me, the one who always pushed me away. 'Of course, we are alike because we are elder sisters,' Hannah had said to me once. 'We had to look after the younger ones.' 'Sisterhood is powerful' was our slogan back in in the days of the Women's Movement, but we didn't mean our biological sisters. We meant other women whose connections with us were not so tangled with our memories, our pre-memories. Even then, 'sisterhood' was as likely to lead to conflict as to comfort and support.

I thought that when I got home I would go and look at the old music I had stashed on top of the piano or put away in a drawer, music I had bought, and some I got from Dad and Granny. Most of it had disappeared, of course, but I still had a few pieces: a much-thumbed hymn book, Dad's loose copies of Schubert Lieder which had been bound in the cheap, coloured cardboard they used in the bazaar, some old English folk songs, a battered copy of the book of negro spirituals which we had sung along with him, 'Swing Low, Sweet Chariot', and that one about dry bones. I thought about my morning walk, the tune that went round in my head, 'dem bones, dem bones' and the way we danced round the piano while Dad played. Where was Mum then? I couldn't see her. She didn't sing or play the piano.

Like the view in the car mirror (a bend in the road, the headlights of following traffic), it was just snatches of the past that were visible from where I was, driving a little too fast perhaps, towards home.

PACKING

When I was seven, going on eight, my mother started teaching me how to pack.

'Margaret Rachel', she called me, using my full name to show the importance of the occasion. 'Now that you're such a big girl you'll soon be going into boarding up in Kodai. You'll have to pack your things up when you come back home from school for the cool season. First you must put in the books and heavy things,' Mum said. 'Where are your books?'

We were getting ready for the annual migration from the plains to the hills. Every year as long as I could remember, when the hot season came, Mum brought out the trunks and began sorting the clothes. This year I wasn't playing with my sisters, Alison and Janet, or keeping an eye on the baby. I was going to 'do the packing'.

'See,' my mother said. 'The books go flat in the bottom of the trunk. Then awkward-shaped things like shoes. Wrap them in newspapers and fit them in carefully. You can stuff little things that don't crease, like knickers and vests, into the corners to make a flat surface. See how I am doing it?'

'Yes, Mummy.'

'Then you fold your clothes neatly so, to fit on top. You can fold skirts into newspaper to stop them creasing. You don't need tissue paper.'

'What's tissue paper?' I remembered dimly hearing a passage read in church, something about being 'clothed in fine raiment and gold tissue'.

'Oh, it's a kind of thin paper.'

'Is it sparkly?'

'Sparkly? No, it's white. We could get it at home before the war.' 'Before the War', 'Home', words which pointed always to distant times and places. When my parents spoke of 'Home' it

27

was always somewhere else. And so perhaps it was for her. Born in Borsad in Gujarat, India, she had difficulties throughout her life in proving her age and where she came from. She had no birth certificate. Her Certificate of Baptism, written in Gujarati, got more and more fragile as it was taken in and out of envelopes and fingered by officials. When she was in her seventies she wrote me a letter, meticulously dated, as her letters always were, but she had put the year as 1907. 'I must have been doing one of those forms about my date of birth, so I had 1907 in my head,' she said when I teased her about it gently.

I can see her now, standing by the great wooden cliff of the almyra, taking clothes from the shelves and looking them over for moth and signs of white ants. 'You can't keep anything in this climate,' she would sigh, just as she did when she was checking the levels of water in the saucers in which stood the legs of the meat safe. No fridges, then. All perishable food was kept in the wire-cage of the meat-safe. Ants could not cross water, though they could swarm over everything else. The little red ones could raise a huge lump on your arm or ankle, but they were nothing compared to the black ants, which marched in columns, huge creatures bigger than my thumb, with fearsome pincers.

The cool weather things we would need for Kodai were laid out on the floor ready to be packed; the cardigans, the vests, the walking shoes. It was hard to imagine that you might ever need a cardigan. The fan moved the warm air round Mum and Dad's bedroom. Theirs was the one room in the house with an electric fan but they never slept there, preferring the veranda where some cool air might flow in towards dawn.

'Good. That's the cabin trunk done.' She closed the lid of the brown trunk with its hoops of bent wood. 'Now you can help with the tin-liner.' The great trunk in the corner still carried labels saying 'Southampton', 'Tilbury' and 'Bombay', relics of that larger migration back Home which took place every five years. Mum opened the heavy lid. The trunk was big enough for a seven-year old to hide in if you clambered over the side and crouched down. 'But you must never go in it because, if the lid came down, you would be suffocated and die.'

I was, on the whole, an obedient child but when my mother

turned the key in the brass lock and opened the heavy lid, I leaned into the trunk as far as I could, feeling the smoothness of the grey metal lining, sniffing the inviting smell of moth balls and wool. Here were the blankets and Daddy's dark suit. He never wore the suit in India. On the plains he wore white cassocks and, up in the hills, on holiday in Kodai, khaki shorts and short-sleeved shirts, the shirts laid out now ready to be packed.

Now I think of it, I do remember one occasion when he had worn the suit. It was a year earlier when we had been Home on furlough for a year. We were living in that cold, cold missionary house in Edinburgh and Dad had to go to a 'posh do' in connection with the General Assembly of the Church of Scotland. All the 'high heidyins' would be there, he said. Mum had opened up the tin-liner and drawn out the suit. As she shook it out of the folded newspaper, there were grey flutterings.

'Oh, look the moth has got in. Oh, dear! Try it on. Let's see.'

It fitted him still. He had kept his boyish figure but there were flashes of white leg through tiny holes in the trousers.

'You can't go like that! You can't go!'

They looked at each other in dismay while we children stood round.

'I know," he said. 'Have you got any of that black marking ink, that you used to mark clothes for the dhobi.'

'Somewhere.'

'If I put the trousers on, you can put black ink on the leg behind and then it won't show through.'

And so he had stood, rotating slowly, while she knelt down and dabbed his leg through the trousers, making sure the ink stain spread widely enough that no white skin showed. 'Now I can go to the ball', he had said, laughing.

In Edinburgh people wore dark clothes and there were never enough blankets to keep you warm at night. Those heavy blankets! I can remember still the weight of them as you curled tight, trying to keep your feet away from the icy depths of the beds. They were white wool, with scratchy blue stitching round the edge which Mum told me was blanket stitch. It was almost the only stitch I was able to do in needlework lessons. But, of course, that was later at school. They thread together these memories.

Edinburgh was where my parents had met. It was a special place for them. I had always known this but it took years for me to piece together something of that story, the story of how I came to be, of how I find myself now in my old age with a large tin-lined trunk in my bedroom, a trunk covered still in old labels, and faintly visible on the top the words Mum had stencilled on it in white paint before I was born, NOT WANTED ON VOYAGE.

I knew that my mother was a few years older than my father when they met. In those far off days she had been in a more senior post in the Student Christian Movement than he had. Indeed she had been on the appointing committee when he got a job as SCM secretary, responsible for the University of Glasgow while she had charge of the work in Edinburgh. In later years certain acronyms circulated like magic formula through their conversation, cryptic references which I gradually decoded. S.C.M., C.M.S., C.S.I. (though I knew that stood for Church of South India) and – most mysterious of all – one, two, one, George Street – the offices of the mighty Church of Scotland.

'As soon as I saw her on that appointing committee, I said to myself, she's the one for me', Dad would say in later years. But she was more cautious. She was a graduate of Edinburgh University, a rare creature, rattling over the cobbles on her bicycle with her two close women friends. The men called them 'the three graces'. And she was already a seasoned traveller, an expert packer. After all she had been seven when she went to the boarding school in Kent 'for the daughters of missionaries' while her parents sailed back to India. She did not see them for five years but six times a year through all those years she packed her little school suitcase and travelled with her big sisters between Kent and south-west Ireland where her mother's family lived.

I wish now I had asked her more about it. She was the baby, the youngest of the five children who survived and her older sisters had been even younger when they were left behind by their missionary parents. Did their mother, the Granny I never knew, hug little Helen tight as she said goodbye to her? Did she walk away down the road crying, as my Mum, that same little girl grown up, did years later when she said goodbye to me and my sister at the same school gate? I don't know. I do know that Mum always insisted that she had a very happy childhood, that she loved school and had wonderful holidays in Ireland.

It was in Tralee in south-west Ireland where they lived, her aunties. They welcomed their sister's children, took them all to their large upholstered bosoms and loved them. They were the unmarried daughters of the Manse with warm hearts and a delight in stories and indoor games. They taught the children card games and even sometimes played cards in the mornings, as Mum told me years later – laughing guiltily as though she could still shock the souls of her long-dead Presbyterian forebears with such goings on. In those days, she told me, Catholics and Protestants were easy with each other, at least in rural south-west Ireland, where the rain fell softly and my grandfather, a clever farm boy from the North who became a missionary, was known to love a good craic. Like all family stories this has a whiff of fairy-tale about it, but I know for Mum in her growing up, the house in Tralee with these Irish aunts, the 'Chestnut sisters', was home.

The only family photo she ever gave me shows them posed in their Sunday best in their back yard. She named me, her first child, after two of them. The eldest, Margaret in the photo sits upright in a deck chair wearing a hat and a feather boa, the others are ranged along a bench, Bella, Bessie and Mollie (was she the one who wrote hymns and was good with the cows? I have forgotten), while Aggie (the beauty) stands simpering behind them, one hand on her hip and a ribbon round her neck.

She gave me the photo one Christmas. 'Thanks so much, Mum. It's great. I'm sorry I never met any of them,' I said. 'Where's our Granny? Your mother?'

'She must have been out in India when that was taken. I'm not sure who took it.'

'That's a pity. I'd like to see what my other Granny looked like since we never met her and I don't think I've ever seen a photo of her. Did Dad ever meet them, the Chestnut aunts, I mean?'

'Yes, of course. I took him over to Ireland the summer we got engaged.'

Because, as all their friends predicted, not long after that first meeting, she had agreed to marry him. He was charming and persuasive. They were very much in love. She had to give up her job, of course. Apparently even the prospect of marriage made a woman unemployable, though it was four years before they could get married. He had decided to embark on ministerial training, so that he could become ordained and go 'out into the mission field'. Only when he had completed his training, could they get married. She had already thought she might go back to India. ('Weren't you fed up?' I asked her once. 'What did you do those years while you were waiting for him?' 'I can't remember, really, I think school gave me a job for a bit,' she had said vaguely.)

At last, they were approved to go out to India as missionaries of the Church of Scotland. Or, rather, he was appointed as a missionary. She was approved as a wife. It was 1936. They packed the cabin trunks and the tin-liners, crated up the books, the wedding presents, the wind-up gramophone with a selection of 12 inch records (Bach's Brandenburg Concertos and a couple of '30s popular songs), the Crown Derby tea set they had been given by his parents, a reminder of the bourgeois respectability he was leaving behind. Until her death his Mother lamented that he had gone off like that to India instead of going into 'Daddy's firm', as he should have done.

The voyage out on the P and O liner was a second honeymoon. They enjoyed the company, the parties, walking on deck and seeing the first flying fish, the burning deserts surrounding the boat as it moved slowly through the Suez Canal. At Aden, when all the officers on the boat changed their uniforms from navy blue to white, she went down into the first hold to get their tropical clothes out of the cabin trunk and to pack away the winter woollies. They wouldn't need those again until they went up to the hill station in the hot season. She would get used to it, the annual migration from the plains to the hills, the packing and unpacking.

'And at the fancy dress party on the last night on board, we went as "the missionary and his wife",' he told the story in later years. She had disguised her good looks in flat lace-ups, glasses and a borrowed skirt unfashionably long. He wore shorts and a pith helmet, which we always called a topee. 'We won first prize and everyone thought it was a hoot. The thing was, next day we were met off the boat by a couple who had been sent from the church to welcome us and they looked exactly as we had. Oh dear!' They would laugh ruefully.

She was a missionary wife now. Did she fold herself neatly into the role? Of course, parents are just there. You don't ask how or why – not until later. She had four children and we have all been expert packers. Sometimes in later years we would fall out with partners or spouses, who thought packing meant just throwing a few things into a bag or who did not understand that heavy things must always go underneath.

And Mum and Dad moved from city to city: the holy city of Kanchipuram, Edinburgh, Madurai, London, Geneva, Chennai, which was still called Madras. She packed and unpacked the trunks and took out the Indian bedspreads in Khadi cotton, the little Madura table with its carved elephant legs, the Crown Derby tea set, the brass ornament which we children had always used in our Christmas nativity plays to represent the 'gold I bring' of the first wise man. She was rarely Home. She was always at home. She still wrote regular letters to me when I was grown up and married with my own children but her life was a mystery to me as I think mine was to her.

When at last in their sixties they left India to go back Home and settle down in England, she packed up the small precious things which she had taken in and out of trunks so many times. She wrapped them carefully in newspaper and packed them into the big trunk. They were to be sent by sea together with the tin-liner and the cabin trunks. Then the two of them set off to travel over-land back to Britain, with a suitcase each. His a nice leather one bought last time they were back home in Britain. Hers a cheap one bought in the bazaar because it was light to carry. They did not book in advance. They were sure there would be local transport and they were not in a hurry. 'They call us the aged hippies,' he wrote on a postcard from Kabul. They took local buses through Afghanistan and Turkey, and when the last bus left them stranded in a remote Turkish village one night, they were rescued by a local taxi driver who took them home to his family and shared food with them. 'We're going to visit as many as we can of the places where Paul went on his missionary journeys,' he wrote. It was 1974.

'Aren't you worried about them?' people said. But I wasn't. I knew they were good travellers. It was being at Home that might be difficult. But everyone said, 'They can settle down now. Enjoy the grandchildren. Have a garden.' He gardened fiercely, found new work to do in Birmingham, took on the little church opposite the prison and worked with prison visitors, sat in his little study writing books, pamphlets, letters to the newspapers. Off to a conference in South America. Taking her up to live in Glasgow for a year while he gave lectures there. His little leather suitcase got more and more battered.

She waited for him, waited on him. Tried her hand at baking bread and making the puddings he loved: she was good at rhubarb and custard. 'And the rhubarb is out of the garden.' Cups of tea in the Crown Derby tea set for all the visitors. So many visitors, people passing through, travellers with news of India. They were hungry for it.

We came to stay, celebrated birthdays, brought the grand children who played with the line of painted elephants on the windowsill and hid behind the tin-liner trunk on the landing in their games of hide and seek. But our lives were so different from hers. Our only travelling was when we went on holiday. 'We've bought a tent, Mum. We're going to France in the summer.' We had our own ways of doing things, which were not her ways.

'When are you going to give up that work at the University?' she asked me whenever we went to visit.

'I'm not going to give it up, Mum. I enjoy it and the children are fine.'

'But what about David? Doesn't he need you at home more?'

'Mum. I'm at home every evening. I don't go away. I'm there for him and for the girls all the time. It's different now, Mum.'

I wanted to hug her thin body, put my arms round her and say, 'I have tried to make it different.' Wanted to say something trite and important.

'Yes, dear. I know it's different but … and I wish Ali was married.'

'Mum. She's got to live her life.'

'I know, dear, but I wish …'

'Next time we come, Mum, I'm going to bring the lunch. It's too much for you cooking for us all.'

'No dear, I'm fine. I can cook for you and your father always says I am a very good cook. He likes my cooking.'

'Of course he does. But I still think it's a lot for you, so why don't you let me help out a bit when we come. I can bring a casserole.'

PACKING

She got thinner. She still wrote a letter now and then but when we rang she would not come to the phone, saying, 'Your father will give me all the news.' She had never liked the phone. She told everyone about the wonderful pink pills the doctor had prescribed for her. She recommended them. 'Just two a day, little pink pills, and you sleep so well,' she would say. Once she went to the surgery when her doctor was on holiday and some young whippersnapper of a locum tried to tell her that she shouldn't be taking these pills, that they were addictive and she might regret it in her old age. 'And I told him, young man, I am *in* my old age and I am not stopping taking my pills now.'

When they decided in their spry old age that it was time to take themselves off into sheltered housing so they would not be a burden to anybody, they had lived in that house in Birmingham longer than they had lived anywhere. But all that practice in moving, in packing, in shedding possessions, came back into play. Together they packed up the house, folded the past years into the compact space of two rooms. He gave most of his books to the College Library. She went through the china and gave all the uncracked cups to the Salvation Army. She gave me, her eldest daughter, the tin-lined trunk with its stencilled words on the top, 'NOT WANTED ON VOYAGE'. 'Well, I won't need it anymore', she said, when I tried to thank her.

'It drives me mad,' my younger sister confided. 'They could have kept a couple of decent bits of furniture or unchipped crockery for themselves. They have got two rooms to furnish after all.'

'They've still got the Crown Derby tea set. That's survived heaven knows how many journeys.'

'Yes, but it's been packed and unpacked so many times and used so often, half those cups are cracked or held together with that dreadful china glue they use. I'm sure it's poisonous'.

'They've kept some India things; look at all the elephant ornaments in their rooms, and the Madura table and the picture of Kodai. They're not going to part with that. They'll be okay in the Abbeyfield. Mum won't have to cook and Dad can have his puddings and they will be in London, so lots of people can visit them. They'll be fine.'

They were. He did enjoy the puddings and began to develop a little paunch, he who had always been so slim. He got more and more blind and eventually was persuaded to get a white stick which he would hold out in front of him as he stepped out fearlessly into the traffic or strode through the underground. He went on writing, his typing getting more and more erratic. He found readers who came in and read to him several times a week; theology, politics, books on Islam, post-modern theory. He went on writing on his battered typewriter. She read novels from the mobile library. 'You know sometimes I read the same one again but I never really remember them, so it doesn't matter.' She got thinner. She took a range of medications but the little pink pills were the only ones she recommended to the other residents.

Everyone knew she would die before he did. It was one of those things that everyone knew that nobody knew. And how could we? Some people said it looked like they would both go on to be a hundred.

They were always having visitors for tea. The tea set was in constant use. She told him off because, half-blind, he poured the tea onto the tray instead of into the cups. He laughed and cleaned his ears out with one arm of his spectacles. It was a characteristic gesture. Perhaps he did not want to miss a word she said. 'Doesn't she look lovely?' he said when I visited once and she had a new red dress.

He had a heart attack and then, a month later, another, which killed him. She did not know how to write a cheque, could not get herself out of bed. We children conferred. She didn't know what she wanted. She couldn't move. She couldn't stay where she was. They couldn't give her the twenty-four hour care she needed. In the end we organised a nursing home. I still feel guilty about it, though everyone said it was a lovely care home and it did seem so.

Now we did the packing. We put her Bible and her shoes wrapped in newspaper at the bottom of the case. We tucked in the little things to make a flat surface and folded her clothes, the red dress he had loved to see her wearing, the skirts and jumpers. They went into a big suitcase. The carved wooden box in which she had kept the family photos, the painting of Kodai, the line of painted elephants, these went with her into the small room on a long corridor which smelt faintly of disinfectant. We paid someone to take away the cheap furniture.

In the care home she got even thinner. She would look past us, her visiting daughters, to see when her son would arrive. She began to be angry and even once shouted at one of her carers, she who had always been the gracious hostess, the charming lady-wife. She made it up at once, of course, patting the bed and saying, 'Sit down for a minute.'

'She is alive, your Mum,' the carers said when we came to see her.

But the order of things was disrupted. Heavy things underneath was the rule but all the rules were broken now he had died and left her.

A few days after the first anniversary of his death, I went to visit her with my daughter.

'I always think it's funny they call it that,' my daughter said as we walked into the anonymous brick building past the notice advertising its name.

'What?'

'Well, "Home". It's not really, is it? Homey.'

We found her in a chair in the communal living room, the one without the television. She sat, withdrawn into her own world, a gaunt figure in a dress which looked as if it might have belonged to someone else, but round her neck a string of the red plastic poppets she had kept from the 1960s.

'Hello, Granny.'

'Hello, dear. I didn't know you were coming. Is John coming?'

'No, it's just us, I'm afraid.'

'Oh. They brought me in a wheelchair to sit here. I can't really walk now, you know.'

'I'm sorry, Granny. Can I get you anything?'

'No, dear. I'm all right. I've just been sitting here thinking what a wonderful life I've had. I had a wonderful husband and four lovely children and now I've got grown-up grandchildren. I've lived in all those interesting places, you know, lots of interesting places. I've been blessed. Yes, I've been blessed.'

Two days later she died. Not one of us was there with her. We all came too late. We stood round the bed where her body hardly raised the covers.

At her funeral, the south London church was packed. The West Indian women all wore hats; nobody else did; there was a sprinkling of saris, men in assorted clerical gear. We had underestimated the number of orders of service and had to ask all the people who came if they would mind sharing copies when they stood to sing the hymns. We had chosen John Bunyan's 'Pilgrim's Song', 'Who would true valour see, let him come hither.'

Home is where you are not and where perhaps you've never been.

II

BEGINNING
AGAIN
(1946–7)

WHERE THE HEART IS

'Home, home on the range
Where the deer and the antelope play …'

Daddy was playing the big black piano, and singing out of a new song book given him by Uncle Edward. Uncle Edward was one of the American uncles. He and Auntie Rosalie lived in the compound and Rachel and Christine loved going to their house where Auntie Rosalie gave them 'cookies', special biscuits she got from America in food parcels.

'Try this,' Uncle Edward had said to Daddy, giving him the music book. 'A change from all those dreary English folksongs you're always singing. Let's have some good American tunes.' Daddy said he was joking.

Rachel, that's me, Margaret Rachel, could sing 'Home on the range' because she had sung it in Kodai when she had gone to school up in the hills for a few weeks during last hot season. 'Give me a home where the buffalo roam and I'll show you a very messy carpet.' Someone had told her that joke at school. There were no carpets at home but there were two special rugs that Mum called 'Turkish'.

Rachel and Chris loved it when Daddy was at home. Then sometimes after lunch he would play songs and sing with them. Even Jane, though she was still too little even to talk properly, would try to sing.

'What's a range?' Rachel asked Daddy. 'What's it mean, "Home on the range"?'

'Well, Rachel, range is like the plains but in America.'

'Oh! So our bungalow is like a home on the range because we are down in the plains, not up in Kodai.'

'Not really. The plains in America are not like the plains in India. They are big, open spaces with hardly any people and there are lots of people here in India – and not a lot of deer and antelope,' he added.

'But there's lots of buffaloes,' said Rachel.

'They're a different kind of buffalo,' he said. 'Time to stop now. Bye, my dears,' and he went off humming 'Home, home on the range.'

When grown-ups talked about 'home' they meant England where Rachel and Chris had never been. They knew about it though from Peter Rabbit and the other books that the real aunties used to send sometimes for Christmas, so when Mummy told them that they were going to go Home they were very, very excited.

'Now the War is over,' she said, 'We can get a boat.'

To get Home they had had to go on a train for three days and two nights and then on a huge boat for days and days. Rachel and Chris loved the boat and so did Jane. They could run about on the deck and had meals in a big room with lots of tables. Rachel was nearly six so she had to look after Chris and help Mummy with Jane because Jane was not yet two and she used to run away near the rails of the ship where she might fall into the sea. Rachel had to chase her and bring her back.

When they had come off the boat in a place called Southampton, they asked Daddy, 'Are we home now? Is this home?'

But Daddy said, 'Oh. No! We have to get on a train now and go to London and then we have to go on another train and go all the way up to Newcastle and then we have to go in a car and then we will be at your Granny's house.'

'Is that home?'

'Well, no, but we are going to stay there for a while and then we'll go to Edinburgh, which is in Scotland, and live there for a while.'

'Is Scotland near to England? Will we have to go on a boat?'

'No. Scotland and England are nearly the same. Mummy and I used to live in Scotland before we went to India.'

When they got to Granny's it smelt different. Outside it smelt clean and cold in your nose. Inside it smelled funny, not like home in India. 'What's that funny smell, Mummy?' But she said 'Shh' and that all she could smell was polish.

Granny's house was much smaller than the house in India and it did not have verandas or tatties to keep the sun out. There were windows with glass in them and doors that shut. The beds didn't have mosquito nets. 'They don't have malaria in England, so you don't need mosquito nets,' Daddy said. 'It's like Kodai.'

Granny's beds were so high that Rachel had to help Chris get up into the bed because she wasn't tall enough. The beds were soft with blankets and big fat pillows and the girls bounced on them until Mummy told them to stop and took away some of the pillows. It was so exciting! Chris and Rachel had their own room opposite Mummy and Daddy and Jane's room.

The bathroom was the best place. It was not like the bathrooms in India. It had a big white basin stuck onto the wall and taps where hot and cold water came out and a toilet which gushed out water when you pulled the chain above it. Rachel had a stool to stand on, so she could reach the chain and make the water rush out. There was a bath but it was not at all like the bathtubs in India. It was fixed to the floor and was big and white and had taps. Instead of getting hot water out of the round can with a cushion round it, you could turn taps and lots of hot water came out of one and cold out of the other – so much water, you could almost swim in it. When you were finished, instead of Mummy tipping up the tub and letting all the water whoosh out onto the floor and out through the hole in the wall, you could pull a plug and all the water glugged down a hole inside the bath. It went round and round like a whirlpool. Chris and Rachel loved the bath.

Jane loved the toilet. One day she found a packet called Lux that Mummy used for washing. It had little white flakes in it. Jane put a lot of flakes into the toilet, then Rachel stood on the stool and pulled the chain and it made bubbles everywhere. Jane laughed and did it again but Mummy was very cross and said, 'How am I going to get another packet of Lux, I'd like to know? There's none in the shops.'

'Is it on coupons?' Rachel said. She knew about coupons. They were because of the War even though the War was over.

Mummy had to get some when they came back from India and they didn't have any and it was difficult because you needed coupons as well as money to buy things. One day when they were living in Edinburgh Mummy went to the shops to buy some bread and there was a row of buns with icing on them at the bottom of the counter. While Mummy was waiting in the queue near the counter, Jane was looking at the buns. They were near her mouth. She took a bite out of one, then a bite out of another, then another.

'What is that child up to?' said Mummy suddenly. She had to buy the buns with her coupons that week, so they did not have much bread but Rachel and Chris were pleased because the buns were delicious. That was after Jane began eating.

Rachel and Chris loved mealtimes in Granny's house. They ate things that they had never had before; butter and cheese and jam, just like in the Enid Blyton books. Even the same food was not the same as in India. Milk was thick and white and not watery and blue. You wanted to stroke it like stroking a soft sari. 'It's the cream,' Mummy said. 'Drink it up. It is good for you.' But the best thing was sausages. They loved sausages, Chris and Rachel. They were brown and round and shiny and inside the skins was lovely meat but all cut up small so you didn't have to chew it a lot. Jane didn't like sausages; she wouldn't eat anything.

'She still has the effects of the amoebic dysentery,' the doctor said. 'Of course, she is younger than the other two, who seem to have recovered well. She will be all right but I will come back in a week.' He gave them all barley-sugar sweets to suck because they had sore throats – streptococci something. 'Off the ration,' he said to Mummy and he sort of winked at her.

Jane sat in a highchair at meals. She would throw her food on the floor but Chris and Rachel sat on big chairs and ate theirs. One day Jane reached out her finger and stuck it in the butter and put a big blob of butter into her mouth.

'Jane put her finger in the butter,' Rachel said. 'She is naughty.'

'Shh,' said Mummy. And she was smiling.

'But you said we mustn't put our fingers in the butter.'

But Mummy said, 'Shh.' After that Jane began to eat.

Granny's house was in the country and had a big garden

where they could play when it was not raining. Rachel and Chris loved to run about and make dens in the bushes. Jane liked the birdbath. Sometimes they would go for walks and picnics with Mummy and Daddy and Auntie Nancy and Auntie Frances. Mummy said they were real aunties, but Rachel and Chris couldn't tell the difference. Auntie Rosalie was real, too, but she was out in India. There were lots of books in Granny's house, which Daddy and the real aunties had had when they were little, and a dressing-up box so sometimes they could dress up and do plays for the Aunties.

But Granny's house was not home.

'We're going to go to Edinburgh now,' Mummy said one day. 'Get your things together, so that we can pack.' She got out the suitcases. The trunks had gone straight to the house in Edinburgh from the big boat. Auntie Frances had a car. They all squeezed into it with the luggage and she took them to the station to catch the Edinburgh train. There were hardly any people on the station platform, no one selling chai, no one sleeping on the platform. It was very quiet. But the girls were excited. Chris tried to do a somersault on the train seat. She was good at somersaults, but Mummy said she might fall off and break something so she should sit quietly on the seat. Then she and Rachel looked out of the window at the green, green hills. It was not like India. There were no people or villages. Just lots of hills and trees. The train still went clickety-click, like it did in India. The wires outside the train went up and down, up and down, until you felt a bit dizzy.

'Is this home?' Rachel asked when they had unpacked in their new house in Edinburgh.

'Yes. We are going to stay here for nearly a whole year,' said Mummy, 'and you can go to school here, Rachel, but then we will go back.'

'I want to go back now', said Chris. 'I don't like this house.' She started to cry.

Mummy said, 'Look, Christine. You can play with Rachel in the garden here.' But the garden was not nice like Granny's. There were no bushes or places to make dens.

'I don't like the garden,' said Chris.

Then Daddy came in. 'What is it, Chris, dear?' he said.

'Take me back to India,' Chris said, crying and crying. 'Please, Daddy, take me back.'

'We will go back. But not for a bit yet,' said Daddy. 'I know. Let's put on our coats and go out. Perhaps we can go on a tram.'

But that night Chrissie cried again and Rachel got into bed with her and they snuggled together under the blankets until they fell asleep.

◆

They were in Edinburgh for a long time. People there were like ghosts. Everyone in the street or in the shops was white and they wore dark clothes, no colours, no sparkly saris. On the street there was no noise of car horns or music, no little shops where you could see bananas hanging up or garlands or brass pots. The sun never shone. The house they lived in was dark and there was a big picture of cows that frightened Chris so she wouldn't go in that room. It was the front room so they only went in there on Sundays anyway, and it was always cold.

Mummy was worried about lots of things.

'We don't have enough coal,' she told Mrs Hill from next door. 'We weren't here in the summer to build up our stocks like everyone else.' Rachel thought she said 'We don't have enough cold' and that was funny because they were cold all the time. But Mummy told Rachel she meant 'coal', the black, shiny lumps which were put into the kitchen fire every day. You needed coupons and Mummy stood in lots of queues to get coupons. When the coal man came, he emptied the sacks down into the basement through a hole in the garden. The black coal went down into the basement, next to where Mummy did the washing and where the mangle was. Rachel loved the mangle and helped Mummy put the clothes through. They went in all wet and came out flat with a whoosh of water. Then, because she was a big girl, she helped Mummy hang them up in the garden or on racks in the kitchen. There were no dhobis here.

Rachel went to school in Edinburgh but she didn't always understand what the teachers and other girls said because they talked Scottish. There was a girl called Jean who said, 'You talk funny.' And pulled her hair. When she got back to the house she told Mummy, 'I don't want to go to that school.'

'It is a very good school and they have agreed to take you in the middle of the year,' said Mummy. 'You'll settle down.' But then they all got ill with something called measles. Rachel had to have the curtains of the bedroom shut all the time but she didn't care because she was ill and lay in bed with her sore eyes shut. Daddy came and read stories sometimes. Chris was ill, too, and so was Jane. When they began to feel better, their legs were wobbly. It was Christmas and they had a tree and Rachel got some books but she still did not feel very well and neither did Chris. Then they all got ill again. They began to cough. Chris coughed and coughed until she could hardly breathe and she cried.

'It's whooping cough,' the doctor said when he came. 'A lot of it about. We could try this new thing called EmenBee. It's meant to be good but I am not sure about giving it to children. Just keep them warm and give them liquids and steam inhalations.'

Mummy said he was kind. She told Mrs Hill from next door, 'He is the son of an old friend so he didn't charge us.'

'That is good of him,' said Mrs Hill. 'If they bring in this new health service they're talking about it will all be free.'

'That'll be the day', Mummy said. But afterwards she told Rachel she was a lucky girl because Mrs Hill's little girl had got deaf from her measles and now she couldn't hear anything and would never hear anything ever again.

It was very cold in that house and it snowed outside so everything was white. Rachel didn't go back to school and they all stayed in bed. Even Mummy and Daddy went to bed. 'This is the coldest winter for years, even for Scotland,' Mummy told Rachel. 'And we have run out of coal.' She filled a big stone hot-water bottle from the kettle. Daddy called them 'pigs', the stone water bottles. They had a sticking out bit in the middle where Mummy or Daddy poured the hot water in and Rachel thought perhaps that was the pig's snout. They made the bed lovely and warm but they were hard and cold in the morning.

One day Daddy came in and said, 'We are going to Granny's.' He wrapped Rachel up in a blanket and carried her out to a big black car which was outside the house.

'A car?' she said.

'It's a taxi,' Mummy said. 'Now settle down'. And she tucked the blankets round her and round Chris, who was there as well, and Jane all wrapped up. Mummy got in and Daddy sat in the front with the driver. Rachel wanted to stay awake but her eyes kept closing. She opened them once and there were dirty white walls on each side of the road, as high as the roof of the car.

'Where are we?' sitting up for a moment from the blankets.

'Going over Carter Bar in the snow,' Mummy said. 'It is very deep snow.' Then Rachel must have fallen asleep again because next they were at Granny's and Daddy was carrying her upstairs in the blanket and putting her into the big bouncy bed. Granny's house was warm and they could have baths. 'Thank you! Thank you!' Mummy said to Granny. But she said to Rachel, 'Some poor people don't have grannies who can help them keep warm.'

When they were back in the Edinburgh house, one day Daddy called the girls and said, 'I am going back to India and you will have to be very helpful to Mummy. You're all going to live with Auntie May for a while.'

'Can't we come with you, Daddy?' Chris said.

'Yes, we'll be very good,' Rachel said.

'No, dears. You must stay with Mummy and help her. Mummy is expecting a new baby, a brother or sister for you. That's exciting, isn't it?'

'Yes.'

So, then they were living in Huyton with Auntie May. Huyton was in Liverpool, though Auntie May said it used to be a village and she still called the shops, 'The Village'. They were going to have a little baby sister and Mummy was staying behind until the new sister was born while Daddy went back to India. In Huyton, Rachel went to a different school, one behind Auntie May's house. Mummy said it was a very nice girls' school but she didn't know anyone there. All the girls played together and when Rachel came they asked, 'Where you from?' When she said 'India', they said, 'Why aren't you brown? Are you poor? Can you skip a hundred times? Why don't you know how to play jacks?'

Sometimes she walked back from school by herself down the lane. She was seven now and Mummy couldn't always come. She was very big because of the new sister growing inside her. One day when Rachel was coming back from school some big boys came and threw sticks. They were trying to get conkers out of the trees but one stick hit her head and she cried. The boys laughed and ran away.

After that their big cousin, John, Auntie May's son, walked up the lane to meet her on the way back from school. John was nice. He wasn't like other grownups. His mouth was a bit funny and he didn't talk much and when he did it was different from other people's talk. Sometimes he would show Rachel and Chris the special things he kept in the basement. He said they were bombs and bits of planes which had fallen out of the sky in the War. He had a dog called Wendy who used to come with him down the lane to school. She was black and white and liked to run and get sticks that were thrown for her. John loved Wendy. Auntie May loved Wendy, too, but she used to say, 'Get that dog out of the kitchen' when Wendy came in all muddy from the lane and from finding sticks. Auntie used to have two other sons. They were called Harold and Robbie but they were both killed in the war. She had their photos on a little table covered with a lacy cloth. Beside the photos was a big knife that was Harold's Gurkha knife. No one was allowed to touch it.

Rachel and Chris had a bedroom at the back of Auntie May's house. It had wallpaper, not like houses in India with white walls. The wallpaper had a brown pattern of spider webs and little lines which they used to look at when they went to bed. Most things in Auntie May's house were brown; the furniture and the floors and the walls and the doors and the bits along the bottom of the walls, which were dark and shiny and had a pattern you could feel with your fingers. She didn't have a compound but she had a little garden with apple trees in it. The trees were much bigger than the house and when you looked out of the back-room window all you could see were branches and hardly any sky. It was dark in the house but Auntie May would not let anyone cut her trees down.

Each night when Mummy had said prayers with the girls and they had sung 'God who made the earth', Rachel and Chris would lie in the dark. The only sound was traffic on the road. There was no music or firecrackers. No one went along the road singing to keep away the evil spirits. So, Rachel would tell Chris stories. Sometimes they snuggled down in bed together and whispered to each other. It was warm when they did that. You had to have blankets in England and they were heavy but even so Rachel and Chris were always cold, even in bed.

'Tell about us in India,' Chris would say.

'Once there were two little girls who ...'.

'Don't forget Jane.'

'Once there were two big girls and a little girl who lived in a house with their Mummy and Daddy. They had a ...'.

'Don't forget Mosey.'

'But Mosey didn't live in the house. He used to come in every day. Anyway, his real name is Moses.' They thought of Mosey, tall and strong and kind. Where was he now? 'There were two girls and a little girl who lived happily together in a house in India. One day, their Mummy said to them, "We are going back to England". So they packed up all their clothes and their toys and went on a big boat back to England. There they had lots of adventures.'

'Tell about their adventures.'

But Rachel didn't know what adventures they had there.

'Do you remember how the monkeys used to come and try to get our things? I am glad there are no monkeys here.'

'Even if the monkeys came they could not get into Auntie May's house because the windows and doors are shut.'

'Yes, but it feels funny.'

And they thought about how safe it had felt at night inside the mosquito nets, like a little house under the roof of the veranda. They often knew what each other was thinking, Chris and Rachel.

One day John and Chris and Wendy came down the lane to School to meet Rachel. John said, 'You have a baby brother.' Rachel and Chris were surprised because they thought they were going to have a sister but they said they were pleased to have a baby brother. Everyone was pleased. 'A boy at last,' said Auntie May. She liked boys. When she was cooking dinner sometimes she used to give big bits to John and anyone else who was A MAN. She used to say it like that. 'Everyone in India will be pleased,' said Mummy. 'They like boys in India.' She hugged them and showed them the baby, who was called James. He was very red and cried a lot and Mummy stayed in bed and fed him.

A boy on a bicycle came down the lane. Rachel thought it was one of the boys who had thrown sticks at her but he was bringing a telegram. It was from Daddy saying, 'Delighted that we have a son and heir'. Auntie May read it out. Rachel thought she said 'sun and air' but then Auntie May showed her the telegram and it said 'son and heir'. 'Why is baby James an heir?' she asked Mummy.

'Oh! That's just Daddy's joke', Mummy said. 'Because he is a boy, you know.'

The telegram boy must have got to know the lane quite well because lots of telegrams came in the next few days, all saying how pleased everyone was about their baby brother. Rachel had to be very helpful and look after Jane and Chris now that she had a little brother and Mummy was looking after him. But Jane didn't like having her hair brushed and she cried and screamed and ran in to Mummy.

It was getting near Christmas and it was too dark to play outside after Rachel came back from school. She and Chris were playing dominoes in the kitchen when they heard a bang in the hall. They ran out and saw that Cousin John had just dropped the big cabin trunk onto the floor of the hall. He smiled at them, as he always did, with his funny mouth, and Mummy came downstairs carrying the baby.

'Thanks, John,' she said and to Rachel and Chris, 'Now that your little brother has been born safely, we're going back to India. Can you start to collect your toys and things so that we can pack them.'

'Back to India!' Chris and Rachel laughed and jumped up and down.

'Yes. Auntie May is going to come with us to help me with the baby but you'll have to be good helpful girls to her and me.'

'Is John coming, too?' asked Rachel.

'No. John is going to stay with some friends.'

'And Wendy?'

'No. Wendy will stay with John. Now go and start to get your things together.'

'Are we really going back, Mummy? To our house?'

'We're going to a different house in a different place, called Madurai, but we are going back to India. It is exciting, isn't it? But, now, please, go and do as I said. I need to start packing.'

Auntie May's beds were not good for bouncing on like Granny's but Rachel and Chris went upstairs and bounced on the beds, chanting with each bounce, 'We're GOING back to INDIA! We're GOING back to INDIA!' until Auntie May came and told them to stop it at once.

III

EAST IS EAST
(2010/1943–4)

DUST

The presenter of the TV programme on the Dead Sea Scrolls was showing some of the fragments found in earthenware jars. They had been discovered by chance in some desert caves. Dust had preserved them. Dust was what they crumbled into. The task of reconstruction was immense. The scrolls were a million-piece jigsaw without a picture to work from. All those pieces, each with a couple of letters, half a letter, a mark which might be an insect trail or might, the presenter said, be 'a crucial punctuation mark – a jot or a tittle'. That was in the Bible, something like 'till heaven and earth pass away, one jot or tittle shall not pass away'.

Rachel switched off the television and thought ruefully that if her head was not so full of bits of the Bible and quotations from here and there she might have more space for what was in the newspaper, which she had been reading and which had now dropped to the floor. But as it was, Bible sayings and lines of hymns would suddenly come from nowhere to her lips. She would find herself making coffee and singing 'Be thou my vision, Oh Lord of my heart' or humming a tune which turned into 'What a friend we have in Jesus' as she put out the rubbish. It used to drive her mad when Auntie May walked about the house singing 'Oh! Hear us when we cry to thee for those in peril on the sea!' Now Rachel herself was just as bad.

It was no wonder. From earliest childhood her world had been saturated with hymns and Bible stories and sayings. Even the family jokes, the word plays and puns which her father delighted in, were biblical or vaguely ecclesiastical. Like the one about the maid who asked her mistress, 'Is it true that we come from dust and go to dust?'

'Yes, the Bible says so.'

'Well, Ma'am,' the maid replies, 'there is someone either coming or going under the spare room bed.'

55

Like so many adult jokes told at the dinner table, Rachel had not understood why that was funny.

On family walks, when her father had to drop behind to do what her mother called 'paying a visit', he would shout, 'Remember Lot's wife.' Looking back was dangerous. Rachel knew that. But, like Lot's wife, she could not help herself. She wiped the salt from her eyes. Time for bed. The trouble with living on her own was that she went to bed later and later. She picked up the newspaper to finish reading in bed. Her younger friends teased her about being so old-fashioned. They read everything on-line now but – much as she loved her laptop and her smartphone – she liked to be able to hold the paper, turn the pages of the book. The pamphlet she had found this morning at the Library fell out onto the floor. 'Oral History Project', it said in large letters. 'If you are over sixty, come and tell your story.' 'Tell your story,' they said. It was all the craze now. The confessional culture, the assumption that it was good to tell all, but also Rachel thought, as she switched off the lights downstairs, memory wasn't like that. There wasn't a story, just fragments, snatches of song, a dot-to-dot puzzle. A handful of dust. Memories rose up unbidden just as the old hymns rose to her lips from nowhere. She climbed the stairs, remembering.

How dust motes danced in the light coming from the glass roof! They rose and fell – an intricate movement. The child in the highchair watched, rapt. Was it a memory or had she made it up, that sense of being outside time?

Rachel had asked her mother about it once. 'A glass roof?' her mother had said. 'Goodness! Can you really remember that! It must have been when you were one – nearly two. I know because it was up in Kodai. We stayed that hot season in a house called Merton Lodge which had a glass conservatory-sort-of place where we used to eat. We only stayed there one year as it was a barn of a place, even though we shared it with the Smiths and the Clutterbucks, so the year after that we rented another house when we went up to the hills. It was Rock Cottage, I think.'

That conversation had been when Mum and Dad were in the Abbeyfield Home. Dad must have been away on one of his speaking trips or to go to some meeting, so Rachel had had a rare conversation with Mum on her own. Mum had gone to open the carved box full of her photos and memorabilia, saying as she always did, 'I must sort these photos'. That day Mum had found what she wanted quite quickly, drawing out a square green album. 'I was organised in those early years in India,' she had said. 'You were a toddler and Christine was a few months old that hot season in Merton Lodge. So I actually stuck photos into albums. Ah! there, it is.' The photo was one of those tiny square black and white ones taken with her Box Brownie camera. The edges of the album pages crumbled a little, dust in Rachel's hands. She looked carefully at the photo and suddenly remembered the house, but only from some later time in the hills. They must have been walking round the Lake. Who was she with? She couldn't remember but she must have been with someone. Dad, perhaps. If she had been on her own she would have walked as fast as she safely could past the water buffaloes rather than stop, as they had done that day, to watch the huge grey beasts. The whole herd were in the lake, sunk down into the water, their glistening black eyes and noses, their swept back horns, all that showed in a sea of water-lily pads. Then, above them she had seen, through the trees, the big house with the conservatory. She had not taken much notice at the time. It was just one of those houses they had lived in briefly on the annual migration to the hills. Every year this move from the plains – red, hot, dusty – to the green hills – cool, smelling of pine and eucalyptus. It was, Rachel realised now, a legacy of the Raj.

'I to the hills will lift mine eyes, from whence doth come mine aid.' It was her father's favourite psalm, his deep voice ringing out in the metrical version, the rich inheritance of his Presbyterian upbringing. 'The Lord thee keeps, the Lord thy shade on thy right hand by day'. Shade in the daytime could save your life. That is why, if you could, in the hot season you escaped to the hills. The bus would rattle along the road, spreading a cloud of dust behind it – on the mud huts with their palm roofs, on the lines of women walking with bundles on their heads, on the cattle standing in the shade of a banyan tree or nosing in a pile of rubbish. Then the steep climb up the ghat; dusty red sand turning first to scrubby bushes, then to green trees, the bus chug-chugging round the steep bends, under the cut walls of cliff with white painted signs, 'Horn Soundly'.

When the bus engine boiled over, as it always did, everyone got out and walked about, peering down the steep, unguarded sides to the shola thousands of feet down. Invisible in the green treetops far below, black-faced monkeys called out 'who-who? who-who?'. At last they were rattling up through the bazaar at Kodai, as evening came down and kerosene lamps were being lit in the little open shops. The air tasted clean, everyone laughed and talked more quickly, drunk with coolness and altitude. Happy to be together, to arrive, to be in the hills. From whence doth come thine aid.

Then a few weeks later, the journey back, down into the heat and red dust of the plains. The missionary houses in the hills would be closed up for another year, the older children would stay on in boarding school. They would make the trip down the ghat in October for the long holiday. Every year there was this migration up to the hills and back. Then that longer voyage back 'home' on the great liners of the P and O. Always the sense of the other place, the other home. Here we have no abiding city.

Now in her bedroom, Rachel looked across to the trunk, the tin liner, sitting massive and heavy, in the bay window with its brass corners and brass lock. Still visible on top were the traces of the words 'Not Wanted on Voyage' which her mother had stencilled neatly onto it in white paint all those years ago when she and her new husband had set off on the boat to start their lives together as missionaries to the church in South India. The trunk took up a lot of space but Rachel would not get rid of it and now her granddaughter had decided it was a good place to hide behind or turn into a counter for when she played shops in her nana's bedroom. The other trunk Rachel had inherited was the cabin trunk which just fitted under the spare room bed. It sat there now, gathering dust no doubt.

On the bookcase were the family photos, mostly of her parents in their old age, still a handsome couple, she realised, though you never see your parents like that; they are just your Mum and Dad. The family groups were mostly of special occasions, wedding anniversaries, christenings. Film was not to be wasted on trivialities.

When Jane, the third daughter, was to be christened, her Mother had chosen the hymn:

> *By cool Siloam's shady rill how fair the lily grows!*
> *How sweet the breath, beneath the hill, of Sharon's dewy rose!*

Rachel had no idea what they meant but the words were magical. She said them to herself as the christening party made its way back from church through the glare and dust. She felt the heat of the ground even through the soles of her new shoes. 'Cool Siloam's shady rill', she sang under her breath. The dust dulled the shine of the shoes.

'You've been very good. You can go out to play now but try not to get too dirty.'

They loved to play in the dirt and dust, she and Chris. Rachel thought of the christening, of her new little sister. But Jane wasn't born until Rachel was five and Jim when she was eight. They were 'the little ones'. So it was always Rachel and Chris in the time before time began. They knew that the best place in the compound was under the kundumani tree where you could find the bright red seeds on the ground and watch the scurrying ants. They knew that if you could beg a small cup of water from the kitchen and carry it carefully outside, you could let a drop fall on the ground and it made a little cup in the dust. A fragile dust-well, a jot on the ground – or perhaps a tittle. But you could not do that too often. Water was precious. The little cups, the mud cakes, crumbled and turned back to dust and were swept away by the sweeper.

Every morning down on the plains you would wake to the sound of sweep, sweep, sweeping. The sweeper with her bundle of twigs. She was bent over the work, which left circular patterns in the dust outside the house, until people walked on it and left imprints of toes and heels or sometimes the mark of chupples. Every leaf, every twig, every piece of paper or cigarette-end was precious. Nothing could be thrown away.

Not a hair of your head shall be lost.

Then the sweeper would come up the back stairs to empty the pots with all the wee and poo in them. If you met her she would pull her sari over her head and step back. She was untouchable. The term 'Dalit' not yet available to her.

Even the least of these, my brethren.

Did the sweeper live in the go-downs along with Big Tambi's and Moses' family? Rachel did not think so. She could not remember. Big Tambi was the best at jumping. He could jump off the second step onto the cold concrete floor of the dining room. He was two years older than she, and Rachel learned from him the bazaar Tamil which was the only version of the language she knew and with which sometimes she and Chris shocked visitors. Tambi and Rachel and Chris played on the veranda of their big bungalow. It was, she now saw from the photographs, a colonial mansion. Her family ate sitting at a table on chairs and slept in beds with mosquito nets; Tambi's family sat on the earth floor to eat, and slept on thin mats, which were unrolled in the evening and laid out altogether on the floor of the family's one room. That was just how things were.

But God loved everybody. She knew that. Each evening they would say their prayers. 'Thank you God for everything, food and clothes, and please bless Daddy and Mummy and Big Tambi and the Aunties. Amen.' Then a song, usually:

> *God who made the earth*
> *The air, the sky, the sea,*
> *Who gave the light its birth,*
> *Careth for me.*

Or 'Jesus bids us shine with a pure clear light like a little candle burning in the night'.

Her parents said their prayers every morning and evening. She had inherited her father's prayer book. The pages just inside the covers were marked with the traces of dead insects, caught by her father who used to clap the covers of the book shut onto the more persistent mosquitoes and other flying creatures which interrupted evening prayers – snap! There they still were, brown marks on the page – like the marks on the Dead Sea scrolls.

At mealtimes there was grace. 'Thank you for the world so sweet. Thank you for the food we eat.' Even ragi congee, which was the staple for breakfast, was better than nothing, which she knew was what many children had for breakfast, and there were always bananas. Even now, more than sixty years later, her friends joked, they had to make sure they had a good supply of bananas if she came to stay. She hadn't seen an apple until she was seven or eight. Perhaps Eve had taken not an apple but a banana from the tree of knowledge. Wouldn't that make the story quite different?

Sometimes they sang a different grace,

DUST

Lord I would own thy tender care and all thy love for me.
The food I eat the clothes I wear, are all bestowed by thee.

Once a visitor (there were always visitors), after hearing that grace sung, said, 'I wouldn't like to blame God for the clothes I wear.' And all the grownups laughed. Children in the go-downs went about naked for the first couple of years – a piece of string tied round a swollen belly. None of them wore shoes, not even chupples.

Consider the lilies of the field. They toil not, neither do they spin and yet I tell you Solomon in all his glory was not arrayed like one of these.

The house was full of going and coming, the lilt of Tamil, the chatter of Indian English, the yah-yah tones of visitors from Britain, men in shirts and trousers, men in white dhotis, men in cassocks. Sometimes a group of village women squatted on the veranda wanting justice because – being untouchables – they had been denied access to the village well, or bringing some family quarrel which the village punchayet could not resolve. Her father would come out and joke with them in Tamil and they would screech with laughter, shifting on their haunches and moving the betel in their mouths so they could shoot a stream of red spit over the edge of the veranda into the dust.

That was on the front veranda. Visitors did not come to the back veranda which faced the go-downs. Moses worked there in the kitchen. The sweeper would pass after her work, salaaming and pulling the sari over her head. Sometimes the punkah wallah came – if there were lots of important visitors for dinner. The punkah hung above the dining table, a heavy strip of weighted cloth with a rope which ran out through a high hole in the wall to the outside veranda. The punkah wallah would sit cross-legged on the veranda floor, his back against the outside wall of the dining room, rhythmically pulling and releasing, pulling and releasing, the rope, fanning the diners inside while he chewed on his betel. Sometimes, allowed to slip down from table while adult talk went on, Rachel and Chris would go and squat beside him, or sit cross legged and leaning against the wall as he did, chatting in snatches of their bazaar Tamil. The sun beat down beyond the veranda, a wall of heat and brightness. When did they get an electric fan? She could not remember.

Moses still survived, a white-haired patriarch of uncertain age, whose grandchildren were computer programmers in Chicago, Sydney and Mombai. The others were all dead now; her parents, the punkah wallah, her sister.

Dust thou art and to dust thou shalt return.

How to make sense of it? The unthinking privilege beside the commitment to love everyone as children of God. How did her parents make sense of it? Her father's predecessor had refused to allow any Indian to sit down in the house. Her parents had not only invited Indians into their home but had Indian friends. She knew they had been in trouble for refusing to join the English Club, refusing to take part in the ex-patriot tennis parties – even though her mother, an outstanding athlete at school, was an above average player, 'Just what we need in the club, don't you know.' The colonial administrators were on their way out. The last English Collector had lived down the road in a huge mansion. None of the British managers of the local mills allowed their children to play with Indians, as she did. Her parents had supported the Indian Congress Party in their struggle for independence and taught her that Gandhi was a great and good man. Her father's early letters back to his family in England, which she had taken out recently and re-read, struggled to describe what he called 'race prejudice' (racism, of course, was a concept yet to be given a name), and how it disfigured even the Church which taught that God loved everyone. And yet, and yet …

Rachel realised that, though she had the newspaper propped up in front of her, she had not read a word. The lamp showed a film of fine dust on the bedside table as she reached across to switch off the light.

'Must do some cleaning tomorrow', she thought.

THE PHOTO ALBUM

Rachel was emailing her sister, Jane, curtains half-drawn to keep the level winter sunlight off the laptop screen, cup of coffee beside her.

Date: 2 January 2010
Subject: Thanx
Tried to ring a couple of times but I know you have lots on and family still around. Got home safely. Traffic horrid on M6 as usual. Thanx for Christmas and for letting me take Mum's box away. Speak soon,
    Love, R

She paused before starting on another email. The slate roofs of the houses behind hers were rimed with frost. There was an excitement of birds round the garden feeders which were just below her line of vision. She liked this view from her upstairs window.

Date: 2 January 2010
Subject: Your prezzie
Thanks so much, dear Bruv, for the copy of the Hobson-Jobson Dictionary. It is my favourite prezzie; I keep thinking of words to look up and finding new ones. Not just the ones we all know, like bungalow and pyjamas. I wish I hadn't forgotten my Tamil. Of course, we spoke bazaar Tamil, didn't we? Not pukka Tamil like Dad – who everyone always said spoke 'Good Tamil', not the usual missionary version. Remember when Chris was in the hospice and far down and she suddenly spoke to that South Indian nurse in Tamil and the poor nurse didn't know how to react to being told to 'piss off' but in her own tongue. Speak soon.
    Love, R

Rachel switched off the laptop. It was the kind of day when she was glad she did not have to go out to work as she had for all those years. Her task today was to sort the contents of Mum's box, which she had brought back from Jane's after Christmas. It was a small box but made of solid wood and stuffed full of photos, so heavy she had had to ask her neighbour to help lift it out of the boot of the car and carry it into the house. It sat now in her living room, as it had all those years in Mum and Dad's house in Birmingham, then in the Abbeyfield sheltered housing and, then that last year, in Mum's room in the nursing home. In all that time Rachel realized now, she had never looked at it properly. It had been just one of her parents' 'Indian Things', along with the line of painted elephants now ranged in size on her windowsill as her grand-daughter had organised them on her last visit. Rachel stroked the wood, feeling the carved elephants and palm trees.

Miraculously there was still a key which worked. She opened the carved lid. On the top were three or four green photo albums which she recognized. She took them out and sniffed them. They smelled of dust and faintly of that room in the nursing home.

In the early days of her marriage when Mum had still stuck photos carefully into the albums with special transparent photo corners (so fiddly), she had written notes underneath in her best writing: 'The Church of Scotland Tea Party, 1937', 'Picnic at Neptune's Pool, May 1941' right up to ' Jane's Christening, December 1944'. Rachel turned the pages carefully. She could imagine her mother writing these titles with her beloved fountain pen, the bottle of ink beside her (she favoured blue-black; no biros then). That handwriting, familiar from so many letters brought Mum before her more sharply than any photograph. Rachel remembered when she had had to go to the bank after Dad died to sort out his affairs. Suddenly a slip of paper in his familiar scribble had fallen out of the file she was carrying and she had burst into tears.

And it wasn't all one way. When Mum and Dad, both in their late eighties, had left the house in Birmingham to go into the Abbeyfield Home, they had given Rachel back some letters tied up in a rubber band, a handful of the hundreds (or was it thousands?) of letters she had written to them over time – blue air mail forms in her schoolgirl hand, envelopes from the early years of her own marriage, letters she had written to them over all those long years of separation. 'We won't have room for them and thought you'd like them back,' Mum had said. But Rachel couldn't bear to read them. She had stuffed them into the cabin trunk under the spare room bed. No longer coming and going, as it had for all those years, including Rachel's time at boarding school, the trunk had now become for her like the Jewish genizah, a place in the synagogue – she had been told – where texts too sacred to destroy or throw away, were stored and allowed to decay, gradually sinking back into dust. She had a few of their letters, too. Sometime, perhaps, before she died she would be able to take them out, the flimsy blue airmail forms, the occasional typed letters from Dad which left a slight purple stain on your hands because he typed multiple copies for all the family using carbon paper.

'Did Mum and Dad give you back your letters?' she'd asked Jane at Christmas.

'Yes.'

'Have you read any of them?'

'One or two. My first one from boarding school in England was full of worries like "I don't know what to do about my dhobi" but after that – well – they don't say anything. Not sure why I kept them.'

Jane was usually the decisive one who was good at throwing out the baggage of the past. When they had gone through Chris's flat after her death, as Rachel had hesitated over the ornaments, the fading photos and Chris's old sketch books, Jane had got out the black bin liner and swept it all away. 'No point in keeping all this,' she'd said firmly.

'I am sure she is right but I find it hard,' Rachel had confided to her brother later.

'Me too!'

'I've kept all the old letters but I am not sure I'll ever read them and besides,' she had hesitated, 'the one thing I am sure of is that whatever they say it's unreliable.'

'Yes, the Pravda style of letter-writing.' He had grinned. 'Everything on the collective farm is working perfectly. The five-year plan will be completed on time.'

They had laughed ruefully while Rachel said, 'You know, only people who remember the Soviet Union would get that joke. It's a seventies joke. We are so old now.' But, he was right. In letters, as in packing, it was best to keep the surface smooth. Heavy things underneath. Some time she would take the letters out and read them. They might surprise her. Memory, too, was unreliable. But not now. Now, she was sorting the photos.

Beneath the albums were fat envelopes with Mum's writing on the front ('Golden Wedding Celebration', 'London, 1996', or 'Edinburgh, 1952') but mostly the photos lay in sedimented layers, not always in order of age but disrupted by past rummagings, so that pictures from the 1940s were mixed up with later undated colour holiday snaps and shiny black and white group photos of unidentifiable people, probably long dead. Some had stuck together and Rachel had to ease them gently apart before depositing them in the 'Unknown' pile.

By far the biggest pile – and growing – was the one she had called 'Dad; Official'. The early ones showed him wearing a white cassock under palm trees or talking to a woman on the edge of a paddy field (this one had been used again and again for biographies and laudatory articles), later ones showed him in meetings, addressing conferences, sitting with groups of important looking men in suits or standing with ecclesiastical dignitaries in what looked like varieties of fancy nightwear.

Here was a blue and white Kodak envelope. Mum had written on the front 'Northumberland, September, 1939'; 1939, the year of Rachel's birth. Small, square black and white photos of a family picnic. There was Dad's family in the hills of his beloved Northumberland, represented here in grey bracken fronds and a black and white stream over which Dad, looking impossibly youthful, was carrying a Moses basket. The bundle of clothes in the basket must be three-month old Rachel herself. Mum, smiling a rather tight smile, was in the foreground of several photos, a handkerchief tied round her head and behind her, the grandfather Rachel had never known and Granny in the long Edwardian skirt and hat she always wore, even on a picnic.

Impossible to tell the weather from the photos (though in Rachel's memory those hills were rarely sunny) but the world was darkening and war would soon be declared. This picnic must have taken place just before her parents had set off back to India. So this was Dad's farewell to this wild place, which he had told Rachel on their last walk there together was the landscape he always carried in his heart. It was also a farewell to his family. He and his father never saw each other again. They must have known this might be so. They certainly knew that, at the best, they would not see each other for five years. Their only contact would be letters, which could take months to arrive – and then only if the convoys got through. Grandad knew all about ships and the hazards of the seas in war and in peace. He had spent his life in shipping, starting as a boy runner on the quayside in Newcastle. Dad had been bought up in a city connected to the world by ships. It wasn't that, of course, which was sending him now to India. That decision came directly out of his involvement in the Student Christian Movement of the early 1930s where he had met Mum, but it owed something to the radical non-conformist Christianity of his family. After all his parents had met at the Presbyterian Church in Jesmond, Newcastle.

And how did Granny feel, in her hat and dark, ankle-length skirt, standing just behind her husband in the photos? She'd been a brilliant young pianist but her mother had stopped her from becoming a professional. She had to make a good marriage, become a respectable Newcastle bourgeois. Even when she had married grandpa her family didn't think him good enough. The large upright piano with its brass candlesticks now rising up behind her as Rachel sat on the floor had been Granny's. She looked, unsmiling, at the camera, her face anxious. But then she was always anxious, even if you were just going into the village to do some shopping. And here was her adored, her only, son, going off to an unimaginable country full of natives of unknown temperament with a slightly gipsyish Irish woman and her first and only grandchild.

Mum must already have said goodbye to *her* mother, who was also to die before the war ended. Rachel had looked for a photo of her Irish granny. But she was not only absent from that photo of the Aunties which Rachel had hung in the hall. There wasn't a photo of her anywhere. Now in an envelope marked 'Henderson Family', Rachel found a grainy shot of a seated woman with a long thin face. On the back Mum had written 'Kathleen Henderson'.

Here was the other Granny, who in the autumn of 1939 said goodbye to her daughter and her grandchild for ever. No phone calls, just letters arriving occasionally with old news. 'Unto the third and fourth generation', Rachel thought to herself. She took out the photo of her Irish grandmother and slipped the rest back into the envelope, which she put into the small pile for 'Family 1939–1945'.

Mum had had a box Brownie she was proud of, but film was almost impossible to get in India during the war or even after it. In 1943 Mum must have got hold of some film and there was a clutch of photos of her and Chris. Their dresses looked identical but Rachel knew that hers was blue and Chris's green. Mum had asked the tailor to make them in those colours as she always did. He had sat on the back veranda with his sewing machine and his clever fingers.

People sometimes mistook them for twins but Rachel was still that little bit taller and she knew already, had always known, that she was the big sister and she must always look after her little sister.

Rachel got up from the carpet and stretched. She had a memory or perhaps it was a memory of a memory. Mum had gone out and left them with – who was that woman in the blue sari? 'We didn't have an ayah,' she had told Hannah, 'we had occasional babysitters' … but which one was this? Rachel remembered her because she was sobbing. Rachel, too, was crying because Mum had told her she was a very, very naughty girl. Seeing the woman in the blue sari crying was a terrible thing for, after all, she was a grown up and perhaps it was that which made Rachel remember. It was all vivid still, the wooden stairs with their open slats and splintery wood flaked with old paint, which led up from the veranda to the flat roof, the fierce heat and light of the sun and the roof baked so hot it hurt the feet, Mum running up onto the roof, snatching Chris up and shouting at Rachel, at the woman in the blue sari who cried. Rachel knew that she had encouraged Chris to crawl up the stairs with her onto the roof. Chris was still really a baby. 'You must never go up onto the roof.' She had been told that so often. 'You might fall off and the tank is up there.' Rachel remembered the slightly rusty square tin tank in the corner of the roof in which the water was baked by the sun for baths. She had not looked after Chris. She must always look after Chris. She must never let go of her little sister's hand. She was three.

Rachel looked for a photo of that bungalow in Kanchipuram, the city of two thousand temples, where they had lived for those first years of her life. No joy: so she looked for one of the house in Madurai where they had gone to live after that year in Britain when Jim was born but she could only find a picture of a generic bungalow.

It looked vast. Of course, the verandas made the house look bigger and half the house we had later in Madurai was taken up with the church offices. Still, these 'bungalows' were enormous by the standards of local housing and they spoke colonial power. Dad's predecessor had refused to allow Indians to sit down in his bungalow. Dad and Mum had close Indian colleagues and friends. And yet, even missionaries like Mum and Dad who supported Indian independence and were critical of the colonial project were still caught up in it, Rachel thought. How could they not be, living in a house like that?

'Another few minutes', she thought, turning over the photos, hoping to find some picture of the compound or the bazaar or the city she remembered so clearly. There was only a battered old post card of a gopuram, one of the great towers of the Temple which dominated Madurai. Of course, Mum didn't waste precious film on scenery. You kept it for people, mainly your family.

'I've been sorting the old photos', she told her daughter when they spoke on the phone that evening.

'I'd like to see them. Next time we're up perhaps. Did you get the ones I texted you?'

'Yes, thanks so much, love. They are gorgeous. I look forward to seeing you all in a couple of weeks.'

How Mum would have loved the way we have photos all the time now, Rachel thought. But would she? The photos in her box had included several of those family groups which Mum insisted on having taken on those rare occasions when they were all together. Several of them appeared in the second edition of Dad's autobiography. Rachel hated them. They looked posed. They were posed. Evidence for the defence, she sometimes thought. 'Look at our happy family all together.'

HOME IS WHERE

That night she sat up in bed to write in her occasional journal.

Rachel's Journal
January 2010
Sorted photos today. A more productive time than yesterday which
I spent trying to buy a pair of trousers. Couldn't find anything I
liked in my size. Perhaps the bad old days of the tailor sitting on
the veranda – or in his little open fronted shop in the bazaar – and
making up the cloth you bought were not so bad. Not that those
clothes were ever a great fit either. Those early days in India when
the bazaar was an exciting but dangerous place where we rarely
went. But, then, we never had any money as kids.

Now she thought about it, Rachel realized that that even in Kodai
they had not been allowed out of school most of the time and down
on the plains everything outside the compound was mysterious.
There the city heaved and murmured and thrust its maimed limbs
at you when you ventured out beyond the shelter of the compound
walls. All those lepers with stumps of hands and the man pushing
himself along on a little box on wheels because he had no legs and
the thin children with huge, sticky eyes and hands held out towards
the white-skinned, rich people. 'Baksheesh, Baksheesh.' Their palms
were pale. We weren't allowed to give and – anyway – we never had
any money, Rachel thought. Like the Queen, I suppose. We were
rich but we didn't carry money. Not an anna. Sixteen annas to the
rupee; a thousand rupees, one lakh, when had she learned that?
Certainly before twelve pennies to the shilling, twenty shillings to
the pound.

She wrote again, scrawling in the large notebook she kept for her
occasional journaling.

When did I start getting pocket money? I suppose when we went
to school in England. I had ten shillings a term, though Granny
usually pressed half-a-crown or even five shillings into our hands
when we arrived for the holidays. Ten shillings, fifty pence in
modern money and out of that we had to put into the collection
plate every Sunday. Of course, ten shillings was worth a lot more
in the 1950s but still...

But her mind was on those days in India, the thrill of going out into the town; the constant blare of car horns, the snatches of music, the colours, the sense of bustle and energy. The roads were full of vandys, cars hooting, rickshaws pulled by men with thin legs, their ribs showing, cows weaving their way through the traffic, and the sun beating down, and everywhere, pervasive as the sun, the stench. The smell of excrement and rotting material. Seeing a man in the street lift his dhoti to piss into the gutter was not remarkable, though she was a bit surprised to see the long brown thing under the white cloth. All those little shops opening onto the street. The distinctive shape of the Temple gopuram rising above everything in the city, a grey mass of carved figures, sensuous, entwined, not yet painted in the bright colours of the Hindu revival. Under the gopurum, the gate into the Temple compound from which the elephant would sometimes come, swaying through the streets to the sound of the drums. Those South Indian drums, insistent background to her childhood, as was the rise and fall of modal music, firecrackers in the distance. The city murmured to itself all day long and all night as she lay inside the mosquito net on the veranda in the soft darkness.

We were protected as children. That paradox of our growing up. We never had any money but we were white, part of the old colonial power much as Mum and Dad disowned it. The Church struggling with questions of equality and difference: difference between brown and white, difference between men and women, who gives and who receives.

Though India has changed a lot, I know, I don't want to go back as a privileged tourist staying in air-conditioned hotels (well protected from undesirables), going round the Meenakshi Temple, then off in air-conditioned cars to Peryar Game Reserve. That's what I don't want if I go back. But I can't want the chaos and corruption and the faeces in the gutter and the man with no legs. How dreadful to want that!

She paused again and thought that, of course, she had done the tourist bit once. She had forgotten until she had started on this rambling writing, which so often now returned to that Indian childhood. Yes, she had forgotten that visit to the Temple she had made just before they set off for Colombo to board the P and O liner back to Britain when she was – what – twelve? Mum and Dad must have decided that before she went home to boarding school, leaving India for ever, she should at least see the inside of the famous Meenakshi Temple which brought pilgrims streaming into Madurai from all over India. She had often enough seen the white and red striped wall of the compound which stood at the centre of the city. You could hardly avoid it. But she had never been inside.

For some reason Chris didn't come on this trip, even though she, too was to be left behind in England when the rest of the family returned. Perhaps she was thought too young to understand. Perhaps Mum was afraid she would take fright at the figures of the gods, which were – Rachel thought now – pretty scary. Chris was still given to 'taking a scunner at' things, as she had in past years – being scared of pictures, or the moon, or that white statue in a garden across the Lake, seen through the trees from one of the Kodai houses.

So who was it who went round the Temple with Rachel that spring before she was shipped back to England for the last time? She could not remember but whoever they were, they had joined the crowds going into the outer courtyard with its red and white stripes, familiar from every temple and sacred place and even from the tree trunks beside the wayside shrines. It was one of the things that felt strange about England. There were no red and white stripes anywhere, just greyness under a grey sky.

They had walked past the huge sunken tank with its green water. It didn't look inviting, though several people were going down the steps. The guide explained about ritual cleansing. Of course, Rachel had always known about the importance of the tank – not only the little tin one on the roof or those in the fields which held water for the villages between monsoons but also the temple tank where Hindus bathed before doing their pujas. It was one of those things she had grown up with. Dad had told her that it was Indians who had taught Europeans the importance of bathing. Before that, he said, our ancestors had sewn themselves into their clothes for the winter and even now Indians thought Europeans were a dirty lot. But bathing here was not about cleanliness, any more than it was in the Bible. Rachel had once refused to wash her hands before dinner because Jesus told his disciples you didn't have to.

'It's quite different', said Mum.

'But why?' Rachel wanted to know. 'Jesus said it didn't matter.' What a pious prig she had been!

At the edge of the courtyard, she and her companions had taken off their sandals, bare feet crunching the bat droppings in the sudden shadow of the gopuram tower. They joined the crowds of women, their saris pulled over their heads in respect, carrying their offerings of coconuts and jasmine garlands into the inner temple, doing their pujas. They were in family groups. One young woman in a blue and gold sari, a fresh bindi on her forehead, moved past, not catching Rachel's eye.

She remembered that much but then memory blurred. She realized now that it was all too much, too sensuous, too full of movement and sound, the huge figures of the gods (filthy idols?), the crowds swirling about the pillars, the chanting and drums and the saffron-clad Brahmins, one hugely fat, taking the offerings and carrying them before the gods. Rachel's guide stopped her and said they should go back but already Rachel felt they had gone too far. She did not know how to see these things. It was so unlike the austerity of the Sunday worship in church or school hall. Here was no order that she could discern, no word spoken to silent listeners, no collective singing in a plain white-washed building. Instead apparent chaos, wild movement of people, the incense, drums, colour of saris. Sensuous, sensual. Yet clearly it was something to do with worship and the sacred. Confusion of messages, confusion of feelings. She wanted to go home – wherever that was now. She could not talk about it afterwards, pushed it back into some recess of memory and closed the door. She had not thought of it for years. Perhaps the post card of the temple she had found among the photos this afternoon, had triggered this memory.

She returned to her writing:

We were protected in the compound, but even inside sometimes, it felt unpredictable, even dangerous, like when there were the student riots and suddenly there were young men rampaging past the house, throwing stones and shouting. What was all that about? Something about exams and people paying to see the papers beforehand or giving presents to staff and then not being given high grades. I never did understand. 'Corruption', was all that Dad would say, 'A different set of ideas about how to get on, not the old ones of family connections and greasing palms which people are used to.' We were told to stay upstairs but Chris and I crouched down behind the veranda balustrade and peered through at the groups of students as they rushed past, arms raised in the air, shouting slogans we didn't understand. They were all young men, dressed in shirts and trousers. Modern men; no dhotis. No women, either.

She stopped and thought for a moment. There were snakes in the compound, of course. The snake charmer came once or twice, weaving his music – like a spell – until the cobra rose and spread its hood, swaying in the basket. He said it would help him to catch the wild snakes and kill them. Did he? She didn't remember. She turned back to her notebook.

But – we were so safe. Easy to think of it now as idyllic. What we had as children was – what? – not the tourist version but still an India filtered through privilege. Of course, we didn't know what we were was coming 'back Home' to in England, leaving the old bungalow for a different life.

MANGO SEASON

It was sorting the photos which sent Rachel to look up 'Indian hill stations' on her laptop. Tucked into the green album, she had found a fading picture postcard labelled 'Kodaikanal Hill Station' along with some photos of picnics, small, sepia landscapes, some dotted with figures. They conveyed little of what she remembered of those May holidays, when the plains shimmered in the heat, but in the hills the air was deliciously cool, scented with pine and eucalyptus, memories encoded in the body which no photo could capture.

Rachel typed 'Indian hill stations' into her laptop browser and brought up hundreds of tourist websites. She tried 'Kodaikanal' and began to scroll rapidly down:

> With its rocks, woods, lovely lake and bracing air, Kodaikanal is an ideal hill resort…It is situated at an altitude of about 2,133m high and covers an area of 21.45km sq …

The prose had that slightly old-fashioned feel which gave Indian English its special – and to her delicious – flavour:

> Kodaikanal is one of the most popular and charming hill resorts in India. It stands amidst sylvan beauty on the southern crest of the upper Palani Hills near Madurai in Tamil Nadu …
> … located amidst the folds of the verdant Palni hills it is one of the most popular serene hill stations, which mesmerises any visitor …

Clearly Kodai had taken on a new life as an international holiday destination …

> Kodaikanal or Kodai is often referred to as the 'Princess of Hill

75

stations' and is a popular tourist destination. International Tourism keeps the city going. Established in the mid-19th century, Kodaikanal always served as a scenic and cool hill station to beat the high temperatures of the lowlands.

The picture on this site was exactly the same as the old postcard Rachel had found in her mother's box. Kodai could not possibly look like that now. Was the use of the old black and white photo a deliberate piece of Raj nostalgia? She found an article in Google Scholar:

> The development of 'the hill station' was a distinctive aspect of British Colonial Rule particularly in India … During the 'hot season' the entire Government of the Raj moved from the capital, Calcutta, to Simla (Shimla) on the lower slopes of the Himalayas … Likewise in South India the provincial government moved from Madras to the hill station of Ootacamund (nicknamed Ooti by the British). Other important hill stations in North India were Darjeeling, where the British introduced tea plantations, and in South India, Munnar and Kodaikanal (Kodai) ….

May was the hot season, the time for staying in one of the Kodai houses – a different one every year. These houses were smaller than the bungalows down on the plains. Instead of verandas and tatties they had windows with glass in them. There were no poles on the beds because you did not need mosquito nets. It was fun having different furniture and things but the houses smelt funny when you first arrived, damp and shut up. Rachel and Chris thought that perhaps Rock Cottage, was their favourite house, the one they stayed in that memorable year when Rachel was eight.

'Is this our house now? 'Rachel asked Mummy, who was unpacking their things into the almyra in Rock Cottage after the journey up the ghat.

'Well, for while we are here. All the Kodai houses belong to the missionary societies and they keep them so families can come up here in the hot season,' Mummy said.

'How long are we going to stay here?'

'Daddy will come up for two weeks, as usual, but I will be here longer, perhaps six or seven weeks, so you can go to school.'

For Kodai also meant school where Rachel had started during the hot season before that year of odd schooling back 'Home'. Mummy had come up early this year so that Rachel could go to school for a few weeks before Daddy and the Uncles came up for the holidays. Classes began again at the end of May and soon after, at the end of the hot season, everyone else would go back down to the plains. Only the big children stayed on at school and went 'into boarding'.

But May was holiday time. Not the long holidays from October to January when school closed and all the children from boarding went down to the plains. This was the short, hot-season holiday when everyone came up to the hills and all the missionary houses were full. Daddy came up, too and there were walks to Pillar Rocks, where you could look down, down to the plains, and picnics at Fairy Falls and Neptune's Pool, where you could swim, and Whiffey.

'That's a funny name for a pool', Rachel said to Daddy on one of their walks.

'It's not its real name. I think perhaps a tiger had left a bit of a dead animal near there once and someone called it that and the name has stuck. It's a joke name, a bit like calling the tracks up from the Lake near Rock Cottage 'Consumption Ghat' and 'Sudden Death'.

'But that's their names', said Rachel.

May was also mango season. Mum always said that a punt on the lake was the only place to eat a mango. At least there you could lean over the side and let the juice drip down into the water. 'Honestly. Look at your chins!' she said to Rachel and Chris. 'You're seven now, Rachel, old enough to eat a mango without making such a mess.'

'Oh, but, Mummy, mangos are so drippy.'

'And yummy', said Christine.

When Daddy was up in Kodai, Rachel and Chris always wanted to go on the lake in a punt. 'Please, please,' they would say but Daddy did not need much persuading. He liked punts too. 'A punt picnic!' he would say, 'What a good idea! Come on you two, come and help choose one.'

The boat house was dim and cool. It smelt of the lake. Rowing boats and punts lay tied up on the dark water and between them were gangways of wood where you walked out to climb into the boat your daddy had chosen. 'That one,' he would point and the boat-boy would get cushions and paddles or oars and a boat hook and jump into the boat, which bobbed around while he arranged cushions. Daddy gave the boat-wallah money and pushed out. You had to keep your hands inside while Daddy pulled the punt along the line of boats, hand over hand, until suddenly you were out into the dazzle of the lake. 'Hello! Hello!' There was Mummy with Jane and the baby waiting on the jetty.

'I want to be in the front.'

'*I* want to be in the front.'

'I want to paddle.'

'You can both sit in the front, but Daddy will paddle until we get out into the lake. Don't lean over too far or you'll fall in.' Mummy smiled as she stretched out on the cushions. She put the baby down beside her and held the back of Jane's dress, who leaned over the edge, laughing and splashing with her hands. Daddy sat at the back and paddled, first on one side then on the other, so the punt would go straight. You could lean over and trail your hands in the cool, dark water. Rowing boats were fast and wobbly, but punts were flat with cushions. Daddy said they had them in a place called Cambridge in England. How punts came from Cambridge to Kodai did not seem strange to Rachel. It was just how things were.

May was also the time for visiting one of the huts. The girls liked Vanderavu best. Just going for a journey in a car was exciting. The three girls sat in the back with all the luggage and Mummy sat in the front with the baby on her knee and Daddy drove. They sang songs all the way; 'The animals went in two by two', 'Green grow the rushes, O' and silly songs Daddy taught them like, 'There was a wee drummer who cam' frae Fife', with its nonsense chorus which they shouted out as the car went up Observatory Road past the golf course. 'Alinqua – rashety roo – roo.'

'Who made the huts?' asked Chris.

'God made the huts,' said Rachel. 'God made everything.'

'Yes. God made the trees and the sky and the animals but people built the houses and the huts,' said Daddy. 'Vanderavoo and all the other huts were made for Government wallahs called surveyors.'

'What's surveyors?'

'Men who went around India making maps for the Government. But when there are no Government wallahs in the huts, we can go and stay there. Though who knows what will happen now with Independence,' he said to Mummy.

'Here we are. Now, come on, you girls; help carry things.'

Food and sheets and clothes had to be carried down the track, over the little stream and up the other side. Then they had to make their beds. Daddy pulled bracken up and the girls carried armloads of green to put on the floor. Mummy spread a sheet.

'I've got bits sticking into me,' said Chris, when they went to bed.

'So have I.' Rachel wriggled around to squash the bracken. She sniffed the sharp scent of out-doors. It was very dark when the kerosene light was blown out.

Chris suddenly sat up. 'I hear a tiger.'

'Go back to sleep, Chris.'

'But it's sort of snuffling.'

'If you can hear something,' said Mummy, 'it's probably only a jackal.' And then the howl of the jackals rose, a terrible cry, quite near to the hut. However often she heard it, Rachel shivered at the sound. In the morning Chris found a huge stag beetle in her bracken.

'I did have something sticking into me,' she said.

Up behind the hut you came to an edge where you looked down, down, to the sholas. Sometimes all you could see was mist. Then through gaps in the cloud you could see the tops of the trees like a green lumpy blanket ready to catch you if you fell. The call of monkeys, 'Who-Who. Who-Who', drifted up with the mist. Far below, the hill dropped again and there were the red sandy plains, shimmering in the heat.

There were no houses to be seen in the shola below, no roads. 'There's no buses or even jutkas,' Daddy said. 'The people who live here are all tribes people.'

'Don't get too close to the edge,' said Mummy.

'It's a sheer drop of five thousand feet,' Daddy said. 'This is one of the highest points in all of the Palani hills, more than 8000 feet.'

Rachel came back to the present and to Google Scholar:

Though called 'hill stations' these colonial centres were typically built at heights ranging from 1000 to 2,500 metres, higher than any of the 'mountains' of the British Isles ... Offering, as they did, a climate more akin to a warm British summer than that of the 'plains', these hill stations became places of holiday and recreation in which the British elite could create versions of the Britain they remembered or imagined they remembered. They planted gardens and parks with imported plants. They built houses on the model of British homes and mock gothic Victorian churches like those being erected in the suburbs of English cities.

She scrolled on, reading in snatches,

British colonial life in India thus moved between two locations: 'the plains', hot, noisy, restless and 'the hills', green, cool and restful. Though rooted in the natural differences of climate and topography, this was a culturally constructed opposition and one not available to the Indians who were needed to service the British and who lived, often in cramped quarters, around the bazaars ...'

Rachel thought of the bazaar with its little shops on each side of the steep road and the jumble of huts around it, of St Peter's Church with its stained glass, and of all the houses built around the lake with names like Claverack, Netherlocharbour and Windsor Lodge. Along from Rock Cottage was the house called 'Bide-a Wee' which she and Chris always ran past because they did not know who lived there. 'It's the witch's house,' Rachel told Chris as they crouched in the bushes. They never saw anyone come in or out. The house was sunk down among the trees, the blue paint on the doors and window frames cracked and peeling. Then there was Bryant's Park which she realized now had been modelled on a European urban park with flower beds and walks laid out in formal patterns. The British passion for planting 'exotics', trees and bushes from the Empire, to make domestic parks more exciting, had spread here, too. The now enormous eucalyptus tree originally brought as a seedling from Australia had been the source of the army of 'eucys' which had become so characteristic of Kodai. Rachel's friend Catriona who had visited Kodai in 2005 had come back saying that the tropical forests which they had looked down on from the heights of Vanderevoo were now being destroyed not only by the arrival of roads and logging but also by the eucalyptus, which was spreading through the sholas just as British hillsides were being covered by the rhododendron brought back from China and India.

Grown-ups said they liked Bryant's Park, though they rarely went there, but Rachel and Chris thought it was boring. There were no woods where you could make dens or climb trees. The scrubby shola of mimosa trees and lantana bushes behind Rock Cottage was more fun.

Rachel scrolled down through another article she had found.

The British also established boarding schools in Shimla and Ooty, though the practice of sending children 'home' to Britain to get their education meant that these often catered mainly for the younger children as Dale Kennedy has shown in his study of hill stations, *The Magic Mountains: Hill Stations of the British Raj*.

That year, the year Rachel was seven-going-on-eight and they stayed in Rock Cottage, Chris started school, but she didn't like it. She would run away and walk all the way home.

'How did you know the way?' asked Mummy but Chris just said, 'I don't want to go to school. I want to stay at home with you and Jane and the baby.'

'You're six now,' Mummy said. 'If we were at home now you would have to go to school. Children go to school when they're five in England. You must go to school,' she said, 'so you can learn to read.'

'You can read to me, Mummy,' said Chris. But she had to go to school.

Rachel liked school. She could read to herself and she started to have piano lessons after school once a week with Miss Ruth. Mummy said to her, 'I think you're big enough to walk home on your own now when you have piano. I'll come a bit of the way to meet you when I can.' So, sometimes Rachel walked home with Chris but sometimes she was on her own. At the school gate she would meet the halva man carrying his glass box. He would open up the legs of the box and rest it on the ground while he squatted beside it, chewing betel. You could see the sweets; pale squares of Mysore pak, and golden jellabies jewelled with flies. Rachel looked but she never had any money and, besides, you were not allowed to buy sweets. She would smile at him and walk fast.

To get to Rock Cottage from school you walked round 'an arm' of the lake. Daddy told her that is what it was called. The water buffaloes lay, sunk down among the water-lily pads, or – more often – they grazed by the road, swinging their huge horns from side to side as they walked, their grey skins wrinkled, nostrils flaring. Rachel would slide past, hardly breathing. Once when she was coming back from school on her own after a piano lesson, she had seen her mother across the lake. She was in a red dress, carrying the baby. Rachel felt a surge of relief. She waved and walked boldly past the great grey beasts, who took no notice of her, as usual. But the woman kept walking and did not wave back. As Rachel got closer she realized that it was not her mother but someone she did not even recognize. She pretended to wave to the empty road beyond and ran past. Rachel never told anyone about the water buffaloes.

The baby was called James and he was crawling and beginning to walk. He had a little chair for mealtimes with his own little table attached to it and he would sit and bang with his spoon. Mummy said he was a good baby. He didn't cry. Sometimes Mummy asked Rachel to look after him. Rachel loved James but sometimes after school she wanted to go and climb into next door's tree house. It was high up in the tallest fir tree and when you were there no-one could see you. Mummy would come out and call, 'Rachel. Coo-ee. Come down now.'

One night James was crying and crying. He cried so much he woke Rachel up and she came out of the room where she and Chris and Jane were sleeping. James was in his cot and he was arching his back up and crying. Mummy was standing by the cot and when Rachel looked at her she saw that she was crying, too, but without making any noise.

'What is wrong, Mummy? Mummy!' Rachel ran in and pulled Mummy's dressing gown.

'James is very ill', her mother said and she gave a sort of gasp. 'I've gone next door and asked someone to go and fetch the doctor. Go back to bed, darling,' and she tried to pick James up but he just cried louder and went stiff, so it was hard to pick him up.

Rachel did not want to go back to bed but then she heard someone at the door and Mummy said, 'Go back to bed, NOW.' So she did. The next morning there was Auntie Rosalie.

'Where's my Mummy?' said Chris when she saw Auntie Rosalie.

'Mummy, Mummy,' said Jane.

'She has gone to the Van Allen with baby James because he is not very well. I am going to get your breakfast today. You'll have to help me and we will have fun,' said Auntie Rosalie. Mummy said Auntie Rosalie was not their real Auntie because all their real Aunties were in England but Rachel loved her and thought she was beautiful. She had white hair and very pink cheeks and she came from a country called Texas, which she was very proud about. Rachel had to show her where Jane's clothes were kept and then where things were for breakfast and Auntie Rosalie said she was very helpful. Then Auntie Rosalie took Rachel and Chris to school and she came in and said something to Chris's teacher, who everyone called 'Auntie Powell' and even came into Rachel's classroom and said something to Mr Krause. Then she said, 'Bye-bye' to Rachel and told Jane, 'We can go home and have fun today.'

At the end of school, there was Auntie Rosalie again. She said to Rachel and Chris, 'Your Daddy is coming up to Kodai and your Mummy is going to stay with baby James in the Van Allen for a few days.'

'Can we go and see them?'

'Not today,' said Auntie Rosalie, 'because your brother is very ill and we need to make sure you don't all get ill.'

Poor baby James. He had something called infantile paralysis.

'Will he be paralysed like the man in the Bible?' Rachel asked.

'We hope not,' said Daddy.

'What's para – pallarysis?' said Chris.

'It means it is hard for him to move his legs,' said Daddy. 'We'll have to say our prayers especially for him and for all the doctors and nurses.'

Weeks later, or so it seemed, James came home. Rachel and

Chris looked at him very carefully but he looked the same, only he cried sometimes. He especially cried when he had to be strapped to his board. The doctors said that he had to have a board with straps for his legs to make them grow straight and James hated the board. He would scream and wriggle from side to side and Mummy would cry and try to make him keep still so she could do up the straps. Eventually he would be strapped in and he would cry and keep on trying to get out but he couldn't. Poor James. But he only had the board on at night-time. In the day he could still crawl and was beginning to walk quite well holding onto your hand.

Then it was June. The hot season ended. Rachel had her birthday and Mummy began to get out the trunks and to sort things ready for packing.

'Now you're eight, we think you are old enough to stay up in boarding when we go down to the plains,' she said to Rachel.

'But, Mummy ...'

'You'll have your friends and it won't be long until October when you can come back for the long holidays.'

'Can Chrissie stay, too?'

'Christine is too little and she has only just started school. I know you'll be a big brave girl.'

Her first night 'in boarding' Rachel lay awake and could not go to sleep. She was in a big room called a dorm. The other girls were asleep. A light came in from the corridor and made shapes in the dark room. She got up very quietly and tip-toed, so as to make no noise, over to the window. It was dark outside, a moonless night with no stars but there was a light from a house across the valley – just one. If Mummy or Daddy or Chrissie looked out of the window they might see it. They were ten minutes' walk away. They were weeks and weeks away. Tomorrow they would go down to the plains. She was here in boarding until the big holidays in October. Rachel thought she could just walk out, go up the road, knock at the door and climb into bed next to Chris. They would cuddle down under the blanket and be safe. But she couldn't. Time stretched out. Something large and hard rose up in her throat. She walked carefully back to bed and lay down with her face in the pillow.

Rachel had been looking at the screen without seeing it. Now she came back to another Kodai website and read,

Established in the year 1845, Kodaikanal then saw settlement by American Missionaries who later set up a school run on American lines, an educational institution that is of great repute today.

◆

'I pledge allegiance to the flag of the United States of America and to the republic for which it stands, one nation under God, indivisible, with liberty and justice for all.' You had to say that every morning in school standing up beside your table with your right hand on your chest. The words were written on the board but everyone in the class stumbled over them, occasionally, even Rachel, who was the best reader. Did 'indivisible' mean the same as invisible, she wondered.

'Rachel, you are not saying the pledge.'

'Mr Krause,' she gulped, 'I'm English, Mr Krause, please. I'm not American.'

'I know you are, Rachel, but you are in an American school and in all American schools we start the day like this. I think your mother and father would have wanted you to do this or they would not have sent you here.'

Rachel did not say anything. She did not think Mummy and Daddy did know, but she would no more speak of it than of the water buffaloes. They would be down on the plains now. She thought of Chris and Jane no doubt at this moment making dust cakes under the kundamani tree or playing school with the dolls. School was not like the games they played.

'Get out your books, open them to page 21 and tick the boxes which answer the questions.' Rachel took her book and looked at page 21. She had done this page already and the next few pages as well. 'James has nine sweets. He wants to share them with his two friends. How many sweets will they each have, 2, 3 or 4?' It showed some American boys in front of an American house. What kind of sweets did they have in America? They did not have jellabies. She knew because she had asked Mr Krause. Yesterday they had done an exercise about breakfast where they had to tick boxes.

Did you have: Toast? Muffin? Pancakes?
Did you drink: Tea? Coffee? Chocolate?'

She could not tick anything. What was a muffin, she wondered.

She did a little fart. Very quietly. But the sweet smell of it enveloped her. Mr Krause sniffed and looked around.

'Someone has passed wind,' he said. 'You are old enough now not to be doing that. Control yourselves.' One of the boys – was it Hans? – giggled softly and got a glare from Mr Krause. 'How could you stop yourself?' she wondered but she was glad he hadn't asked who had done it or she would have had to confess.

Her friend, Ruthie, had made a calendar of all the days until the holidays. Every morning she crossed off the day before. Rachel decided to make a calendar and begin counting the days.

'Close your workbooks now. We are going to do some history. Do you remember what we were talking about last week?'

'Yes, Mr Krause. About how the brave American soldiers fought against the British redcoats and about George Washington who would never tell a lie.'

'Yes, Rachel, we are learning about how the Americans got their independence from the British, which is why America is the land of the free. And today we are going to read a poem about some other brave Americans, it is called 'Paul Revere's Ride'.

> *Listen, my children, and you shall hear*
> *Of the midnight ride of Paul Revere.*

Rachel could still recite chunks of it. It was part of the flotsam which washed around in her brain, along with all the biblical passages and hymns and the poems she had learned by heart in the school in England where she was sent later and where, confusingly, she was to find the British were heroes not villains and George Washington hardly figured in the history lessons.

She found a different article:

These hill stations have also provided the locations for many Bollywood films. The landscapes which were so important in the imagination of the British Raj are thus being recreated in the fantasy life of a vast new population, the descendants of those whom the hill stations were designed to exclude.

Tears, or perhaps the light slanting onto the screen from the window, blinded her. She turned off the laptop and stood up to stretch. In the suburban street below, her neighbour came out of his house and got into his mini cab.

A blue sky over the Manchester rooftops promised a perfect summer day. She made herself a coffee and took it into the garden. The Albertine rose she had planted on the wall was just coming into its best, a mass of pink buds getting paler as they opened, until the almost white petals fell from the blown roses. She sat on the bench, thinking about Kodai. The feel of the air, warm with an undercurrent of coolness, the smell of greenness. They were present to her still after so many years.

Why did she find it so hard to go back? Half her friends went to India now on holiday.

'Come with us to Goa next winter,' Isobel had said over the phone last week. 'We've found this great hotel near the beach. Really cheap. What do you mean, "Goa isn't India"? Oh, well! Suit yourself.' She'd put the phone down.

Rachel knew she was offended. She couldn't explain to herself, let alone to her friends. India hovered before her like the figure of the woman across the lake she had mistaken once for her mother, as she had walked back from school past the water buffaloes. She knew that, if she went closer, the figure would turn into a stranger. No! It was early June now. It was the mango season. She would go out and take the bus to 'Curry Mile' in Rusholme. She would walk past the sari shops, past the pyramids of Mysore pak in the Sweet Emporium, past the take-away selling hallal pizza, and at the greengrocers on the corner she would buy a box of those perfect yellow fruit sold here as 'Pakistani mangos'. She would eat them and let the juice run down her chin.

IV

TRANSITIONS
(2010/1946,1951)

THE INVISIBLE THREAD

Books! She had so many of them, on shelves in every room, stacked on the floor of the bedroom. Of course she read on the screen, scanning the paper on the phone as she went into town on the tram but she still bought the print copy and she still bought books. But she did not have room for anymore and she must move the pile from the floor by the bed. She had already got rid of so many, given some away and sent some to the Oxfam shop but now she must get rid of more.

Rachel couldn't remember a time before she could read. 'Auntie Powell', the teacher in grade 1 at Kodai, who had taught generations of children to read, had not taught her. She was reading before she started school. She had fallen into books, as a fledgling falls off the branch into the air, which is its element.

I'll start with the children's books, she thought. On a shelf were a few kept from her own childhood and some from her children's. For years she had said to herself she was keeping them in case there were grandchildren but now she knew she kept them for herself. Her grandchildren had their own books, all those wonderful children's books which had come out during the last twenty years. She started leafing through the slightly dusty volumes, flooded with memories. Her sixth birthday – or was it her fifth? The first she could remember and what she remembered was sitting on Dad's knee as he gave her a flat brown-paper package.

'What is it?'

'Let's open it and see. I'll undo the knots for you.' He held her carefully while he undid the string, making it into a figure of eight so that it could be put away in the string bag. She slid off his knee and squatted on the floor, unwrapping the brown paper. Inside was a slim paper-backed booklet with a bright green cover and a jagged pattern of triangles in black. No, it was two, three, four, five, *six* booklets in different shades of blue and green, all with a similar pattern on the front.

'Are they for me?' she asked. 'For my very own?'

'Yes.' Daddy and Mummy both smiled at her. Chris picked one up and turned it over. 'But you can share them with Chris,' said Mummy quickly.

'See,' Daddy took her on his knee again and opened the first booklet, 'here's a poem by Rudyard Kipling. He's the man who wrote *Just So Stories*, that you like so much.

> *I keep six honest serving men.*
> *They taught me all I knew.*
> *Their names are What? and Why? and When?*
> *And How? and Where? and Who? ...'*

That's like you, isn't it? Now these books will help answer all those questions you are always pestering grown-ups with.' He was smiling and she knew he really did not mind all the questions. 'Look. This one is *How?*.'

'We like the *Just So Stories*, don't we, Chris?' Rachel said. 'How the elephant got its trunk.'

'Yes, cos of its satiable curtiosity,' said Daddy laughing. 'Just like you.'

Books had been scarce in her childhood, though Dad's office was lined with them. But the office, though in the same building, was entered by a different door and was somewhere she didn't go and, besides, these were boring books. Sometimes as a treat she and Chris had been allowed to get out the illustrated Old Testament, a vast tome bound in white with gold lettering, too heavy to hold. They lay on the floor on their stomachs side by side and turned the pages, savouring the colours and glossy paper. Here was Moses lifting up the golden serpent while all around men and snakes writhed together on the ground, Absalom caught in a thicket by his hair and about to be murdered by men with huge swords, the priests of Baal cutting themselves with their knives and streaming with blood. Was it just that she remembered the blood and gore or was it really so gruesome? Rachel thought of the narthex of a basilica she had visited in Greece where the lives of the martyrs were shown in a detail at once stylised and disturbing. The almost sado-masochistic delight in blood and violence was one disturbing aspect of the Christian tradition which could not be described as a simple opposition between an Old Testament all about judgement against a New Testament all about mercy. She doubted now whether Mum and Dad had ever really looked at the pictures which so engrossed them as children.

Chris's favourite picture was the Death of Jezebel because there were three dogs in the bottom corner licking up Jezebel's blood. Chris was fascinated by the idea of dogs. When Rachel began to read for herself she especially liked George in the *Famous Five* books, partly because she had a dog called Timmy, but of course no one they knew had a dog. Real dogs were scavengers who roamed through the compound in packs with their ribs showing. Dogs were dangerous and could go mad. They foamed at the mouth (Rachel imagined something a bit like Daddy's chin when he was shaving) and if they bit you, you would die horribly. Once someone had run through the compound shouting 'Mad dog! Mad dog!' and Mummy had told them to come in off the veranda where they were playing and go upstairs, while Mosey ran to pull to the veranda doors, which were never closed in the daytime.

Rachel came back to the present and the battered copy of *Peter Rabbit* she had absent-mindedly picked up. Because, after, all, they did have their own books, she and Chris, which were then handed down to the younger ones, Jane and Jim. Their English Aunties, whom they had never seen, managed to send some books out to India even during the war. Parcels didn't always arrive and Christmas presents sometimes turned up in February but then it was so exciting opening them and looking at the pictures of Peter Rabbit in a little blue coat or Mrs Tiggy-Winkle, who Mummy said was a kind of woman dhobi. The copy in her hand was not the one they had unpacked in one of those exciting parcels. It was one she had bought for her own children but the smell and feel of the small, almost square, volumes recalled the intensity of those early encounters. Shiny white paper surrounded pictures of strange animals; rabbits, hedgehogs and ducks, exotic beasts, who lived in that distant country called 'home'. It never occurred to her to ask if animals really wore clothes in England. Information was not what books gave you in those early days. Beatrix Potter's books, like hymns and the Bible, opened up the magic of language. They gave you words to roll on the tongue, to chant and incorporate into games.

'Tiggy-winkle' was a nice word. So was 'soporific', which came in Peter Rabbit. Rachel had gone around for days saying to Chris, 'Soporific! I feel soporific!'

'So terrific?'

'No. Soporific. It's what happens when rabbits eat lettuce.'

'What letters?'

'Lett-**ice.** Not letters.'

'What's that?

'I don't know. Something they have at home. In England.'

Soporific was like the words in the *Just So Stories* that Daddy read them if he was at home when they were going to bed, before they said their prayers. Rachel and Chris would join in, chanting when he got to the best bits, like 'the great grey-green greasy Limpopo River all set about with fever trees'. That was where the crocodile lived who pulled the elephant child's nose. Of course, they didn't understand everything, especially not what the bi-coloured-Python-Rock Snake said, but the words were intoxicating.

'The crocodile didn't really pull the elephant's nose, did it?' Rachel had asked one day soon after her sixth birthday when they were watching the temple elephant swaying down the road alongside the compound. They didn't often see this elephant but sometimes it would come out with the red and white marks of Brahma on its forehead and walk through the city. People would jostle round it to offer coins, which it took delicately in its trunk and passed up to the man sitting between its huge ears. Rachel and Chris could only watch. They weren't allowed to give the elephant anything.

'No. I think it's just a made-up story,' Mummy said. Rachel was not surprised or disappointed. For as long as she could remember she had understood that the world which books opened out to her bore a close but tangential relationship to the everyday world. She had come to understand that there were different kinds of books and, though she did enjoy the 'What?', 'Why?' and 'Where?' books, they were never her preferred reading. Now she could read for herself, she wanted story. Narrative that carried you along into its own secret world.

When the family came back to England, soon after Rachel's sixth birthday, she had discovered there were lots of books for children and she learned to read to herself. The world of print opened out and its landscape changed, a transformation as great as the change from South Indian sunshine to grey northern skies. Reading became something private. Words on the page had no sound. When you read to yourself you didn't even need to say the words in your head. Instead you could surrender yourself to the stream of story. Rachel discovered Enid Blyton. Those old Enid Blyton books, which had been paperbacks with broken spines and curling pages, had disappeared, leaving no material trace but they had carried her into the reading world she had inhabited ever since. Auntie Nan had given her a brand new copy of *Five Go Adventuring Again* and she read it the whole way through. Her first whole book! She experienced for the first time that losing yourself in the story, which was to become an addiction. It was enthralling. Rachel loved George because she was brave, even braver than the boys and, of course, she had Timmy, the dog, but it was the pull of the story, it was wanting to know what happened next, and having that want satisfied, which gave her the high she now began to seek out like any other addict. The 'Again' in the title told Rachel there were other books. She needed them.

In Liverpool where they all went to live with Auntie May for a while, the doctor's wife said she could borrow some of her daughters' books. They had so many and 'They're not great readers, my girls,' she told Auntie May. Rachel returned from their house; her arms full. Then someone from the Church came round with a cardboard box of books. 'My children are too old for these now,' she said to Mummy. 'Do you think your girls might enjoy them?' It was as good as a picnic with lemonade and ham sandwiches. Exotic food of the imagination.

Not that the delight in language disappeared. At Granny's house, the Aunties let her read an old copy of a book of poems called 'The Jumblies', which *they* had read when they were girls. 'Their heads are green and their hands are blue and they went to sea in a sieve, they did.' Rachel and Chris had chanted it together. Rachel looked along her shelves and found her aunts' copy of Edward Lear's poems. The cover was falling off and it opened to 'The Owl and the Pussy Cat'. And, there, next to it on the shelf, of course, was Walter de la

Mare. Rachel opened the copy of Peacock Pie which she had taken everywhere with her since she was seven. The smell of the stiff white paper, the strange little line drawings, still opened onto a world of magic. She leafed through looking for the poem that begins,

> *Is anybody there? said the traveller,*
> *Knocking at the moonlit door …*

but she must have misremembered because it wasn't in this book. She put the books back onto the shelf. She could not get rid of them. Her children would have to do it when she was dead.

Her childhood diet, Rachel realised now, looking back, had been a mix of junk food and solid fare. But all of them had fed her appetite for story, for the excitement of what happens next. The Enid Blytons had disappeared over the years but she still had the volumes of the Victorian and Edwardian classics which had continued to arrive from the real aunties throughout her childhood. She wished now she had said 'thank-you' to them for all those parcels but she had never thought to do so. With the solipsism of childhood she had simply assumed that was what aunts were for. Rachel took from the shelf The Treasure Seekers and The Railway Children in their worn blue covers. How skilfully E. Nesbit carried you into a world where the magical was entirely possible – indeed sometimes awkward and hard to manage like the bad-tempered Psammead in *Five Children and It*.

Was there some other appeal these stories had for her, something beyond simply the delight in narrative? Like Enid Blyton's Famous Five, Nesbit's Edwardian children had parents who left them with careless relatives or compliant servants, so that they could carry on their adventures without adult interruptions. The fantasy of a world in which children always managed to escape from the difficulties had wide appeal for children but perhaps it was the safety of that world from which adults had withdrawn that spoke particularly to those like Rachel whose parents sent them to boarding school early and who 'left them behind' in England when they went out to rule, make money from, or convert the Empire.

When Rachel was in her English boarding school all her friends loved the *Chalet School* stories, but Rachel had never enjoyed them. Perhaps for her the reality of boarding school was too powerful to allow space for such fantasies. The ritual midnight feast, which you had to have at the end of term, had never appealed to her, though she knew that it was given in the script of such stories and was meant to be very exciting and naughty. Perhaps it was because Rachel was too much of a 'good girl' to enjoy being naughty but, no, looking back, she felt that the reality of school blocked out for her the fantasy of the school story. She needed something distant, a world far removed from the world of lessons and schoolgirl relationships. By the time she was twelve or thirteen she had found what she needed elsewhere, still devouring narrative but now in the form of nineteenth-century classics like Walter Scott's *Ivanhoe* or contemporary historical romances like those of Jean Plaidy.

Next to *The Railway Children,* Rachel now saw George Macdonald's *The Princess and the Goblin.* She picked it up and leafed though, looking for the illustrations. Here the Princess made her way up the winding stairs to the top of the tower where the old woman, spinning the invisible thread, waited for her. There Curdie, the miner lad strode forward braving the misshapen goblins who, Chris had feared, might lurk in the dark corners of the veranda at bedtime. The old woman in the tower appeared to the young Princess as a magnificent Queen but seemed a heap of rubbish to Curdie's sceptical eye. So, too, the adult Rachel could no longer see the magic of the pictures, however hard she looked at the glossy paper with its soft-focus colours. Rachel and Chris had loved the story of the goblins and the invisible thread which the grandmother gave the Princess and which could guide you through the darkest place if only you kept your finger on it. They had never connected the figure of the blackened working-class boy, companion to the white Princess, with their Indian playmates. Nor, of course, thought Rachel turning the pages, had they any sense of the theological significance of George MacDonald's images of the old woman in the tower and the invisible thread. To the child she had been, the idea that the old woman might represent God was impossible. God was obviously a man, just like Daddy only bigger and stronger. Still, the idea of the invisible thread which led you safely through all danger still evoked in her a glimmer of childish longing for that image of absolute safety in the face of horrors.

It was when she was thirteen and her parents had gone back to

India leaving Rachel and Chris in England that Rachel fully realised that reading was her own invisible thread which guided her through all difficulties. The School Library was full of nineteenth-century classics in standard editions. She discovered them in her first term, all those old favourites she had here so many years later, but now in battered paperback editions rather than the school library's solid volumes. She remembered going into the Library and taking out an old red copy of *Jane Eyre* with gold lettering on the spine. She had sneaked it into Prep, done her homework very fast and then tried to read it under the desk, only to have it confiscated. She had always been inept at the minor transgressions of boarding school life. Fortunately, she then got ill.

Rachel looked out of the window, memories of her first year at her English school coming back to her with a clarity which caught her by surprise. She could almost smell that mixture of eucalyptus, soap and something else – was it cabbage? – which pervaded the sick bay. 'Isolation,' the doctor had said. Everyone at school knew there were benefits in being ill. Sister in her white uniform liked to listen to the radio in the morning, so Rachel heard a new kind of music. Not the Palm Court Orchestra of Sunday afternoons in Auntie May's front room but the relentlessly up-beat sounds of Workers' Playtime. 'Isolation' for Rachel meant more time to read, at least as soon as Sister said she was well enough and could have books from the Library. Rachel could not now remember how the books got to her in bed in the sick bay but even now when she re-read *Jane Eyre* she felt again a sweaty absorption produced in part by Charlotte Bronte's prose but also by that first tonsillitis-infected reading.

'Anything else by Charlotte Bronte,' she had asked for and got *Wuthering Heights,* which she also read with feverish speed. Heathcliff loomed through her dreams. Rachel was used to being at school with boys. Now, aged thirteen, as tall and as fully developed as she would ever be, she was in an all-female environment during term and during the holidays. She had not a single male relative in Britain. Reading gave her a way of dealing with the sexuality that she could never talk about or even think about outside the world of fiction. *Ivanhoe. Redgauntlet.* She gobbled up the works of Walter Scott, stuffing down great lumps of prose. Thomas Hardy, next, at a slower pace. She got better. She got ill again. She read as if her life depended on it, as perhaps, she thought – looking back – it did.

She had her tonsils out the Easter of the year she was fourteen and suddenly she stopped being ill. But she did not stop reading. It was her lifebelt; it kept her afloat through her teenage years. Not that the idea of being a 'teenager' had been invented then, of course.

'That child always has her nose in a book,' Auntie May would say when they were in Huyton for the school holidays. 'And as for Chris, she is always moping around doing nothing. Go out and get some fresh air.'

But getting fresh air was not easy. Lorries thundered by the house on their way into Liverpool. Rachel and Chris would walk up to the Library together but they did not say much. Chris seemed far away most of the time and Rachel was thinking about her next book.

'I've got us both tickets for the Adult section,' she confided in Chris as she went to take out the next volume in the Jalna series by Mazo de la Roche. With their pink and black covers, Rachel thought they were wonderfully shocking and took the paper covers off when they got home, so that Auntie May wouldn't see them. Chris would wonder round the Library without taking out a book. She wasn't interested in reading. She wasn't interested in anything, really. She did not want to get up in the morning and would sit staring into space until Auntie May told her to go and tidy her room or go out and get some fresh air.

The only people their own age Auntie May knew were the doctors' children and sometimes Rachel and Chris would be invited round to play in their huge garden, but they had their ponies and their other friends and Rachel had read all their books – at least the ones which were interesting.

'Weren't those holidays at Auntie May's awful,' Chris had said to Rachel when they were sitting together in the hospice dayroom where Rachel had wheeled her for a break from the ward. 'There was nothing for us, was there? We were – I don't know – May wasn't horrible to us, but she didn't know what to do with us, did she? She would have preferred a dog.' She paused. 'Looking back now I think that is when I began to be depressed. I think that is when the OCD started, you know.'

'I am so sorry, Chris, darling. I don't think I looked after you very well, did I?' Rachel had said. 'I was too busy reading.'

Chris had smiled. 'You always were a bookworm,' she said.

Rachel turned from the bookshelves to lean on the windowsill of her study-cum-spare bedroom. Water glistened on the rooftops. Suddenly a shape appeared in the space between the window and the house behind, huge, flying slowly with jagged wings, a heron. It must have come up from the river looking for ponds in back gardens, her bird bath a mere gleam in his eye. Rachel held her breath, leaned forward to watch the slow, laboured flight. Then it was gone.

WHERE ARE YOU FROM?

'So. Visiting are you?' the taxi driver asked as they swung out of the station.

'No, no!' she said. 'Coming home.'

'You don't sound Manchester.'

'No.' She never tried to explain about India, all the different schools, the different accents she had adopted to fit in as a child: bazaar Tamil, Edinburgh English, American slang, the Received Pronunciation of her Kent boarding school. 'Been living here forty years,' she said.

'Me too, all me life. Mum and Dad came here nearly fifty years ago, from Pakistan. Still go back in the summer, but … I'm Manc, me.'

Rachel didn't feel like chatting. The train had been crowded and she was tired, glad when at last she was pushing open the door of her house, picking up the post from the floor and going into the kitchen to make a pot of tea.

'And you shall declare before the Lord your God, a wondering Aramean was my father.' One of those Bible sayings that rose unbidden into her mind these days floated up into consciousness. Of course, she had heard it read as part of the lesson recently. It had jolted a memory, a scene from her childhood had flashed into her mind, a shepherd with a ragged flock of those skinny Indian sheep that looked more like goats. He was walking along by the railway track in a cloud of dust, a staff in his hand. Very biblical, she now thought. And Dad was telling her not to lean out of the train window.

She left her case in the hall and went to look in the fridge. She would need to do some shopping but there was enough milk for a cup of tea. Those Indian train journeys were still vivid to her. First, there was the uproar of the station, packed with people shouting, pushing, passing luggage over the heads and round the bodies of others. It was always a little frightening. She had to hold on tight to Chris's hand, so that Chris wouldn't get lost, and clutch hold of Dad's trousers or Mum's skirt as they pushed their way through. Then, the safety of the second-class carriage with its worn seats. Were they really black leather as she remembered? Certainly something a lot more comfortable than the slatted wooden benches of the third-class carriages with their heaving cargo of men, women, children, chickens, bedrolls and bundles wrapped in cloth. Rachel remembered going through the carriage holding Daddy's hand. But the men and women there, chewing their betel and sitting on their bedding were better off than the boys who rode the outsides of the train or even climbed onto the roof. She had seen them jumping down at the station. She was glad she could ride in the second class.

While everyone was still getting settled, there was the long blast on the whistle, the whoosh of steam and the slow pull out of the station, with people running along beside the carriages, trying to complete their last-minute sales through windows. As the train settled into its regular clickety-click, clickety-click, you could look out of the window, feel the hot wind on your face, watch the brilliant green paddy fields, the palm trees, the villages rolling past with their mud huts, roofed in dried palm leaves. Sometimes ragged children waved from near the track and were gone before Rachel had time to wave back. Then the pandemonium of another station seen from the safety of the carriage, with vendors shouting 'Chai! Chai!' above the press of people.

The best bit was at night when the back of the seat was pulled out and hooked up at the side to become another bunk, the luggage was cleared from the top shelf and put on the floor and suddenly, magically, there were three bunks, one above the other along each side of the carriage You unrolled the folded bedding and lay in the flickering dark, listening to the regular beat of the train, which sounded almost inside your head as you lay with your ear to the seat, clickety-click, clickety-click, broken only by the occasional rumble as the train crossed a bridge.

Rachel had fallen into a reverie as she sometimes did these days. A sign of old age, perhaps, or of not having to be always busy, always looking at the clock and checking the diary as she had for most of her life. She was thinking of one particular journey as she sat in the kitchen drinking tea. She thought it was when they had just got off the boat at Bombay (now Mumbai). They were on their way back from England with their new baby brother and had made the three-week voyage from Liverpool. Dad had met them off the boat and they had been plunged back into the heat and colour and din of India. It was, she remembered, like getting the blood back into a cramped limb. The grown-ups were distracted and taken up with their own problems but she and Chris had run about like puppies, sniffing the spicy air, delighted with the journey through the streets so comfortingly noisy and full of traffic and excitement unlike the roads of Edinburgh or Huyton. The house where they spent a day between getting off the boat and catching the train, a house belonging to some friend of Mummy and Daddy's, delighted them. They were going to catch a train and would be on the train for two whole nights and three days, Daddy said. It would take them that long to get to their new home in Madurai.

It was, she remembered, the second day on the train. They had a carriage to themselves, the seven of them, counting Baby James and Auntie May, who had come out to India with them. Rachel and Chris took no notice of her and she sat quietly in the corner all the time. Not like her really but they were too busy to notice. Dad had got off at a station while Rachel and Chris leaned out of the carriage window, longing for the forbidden sweets, drinks of chai or bottled drinks which the vendors on the crowded platform pressed on passengers. The man selling chai poured a brown stream between one glass and another. One of Dad's jokes was about a man who asked for 'a yard of chai'. Beside the man, the used glasses were stacked up, festooned with flies, and a boy Rachel's age squatted beside him slowly wiping the glasses with a dirty rag which, now and then, he dipped into a bucket. Rachel had never worked out how to pour the liquid straight from the glass down your throat without touching your lips to the rim as the men on the platform were doing. Indeed, in the year in England she had forgotten that this was how you drank in India.

Beside the chai seller, two men had a little primus stove going on the platform and were cooking pakora. The scent drifted into the carriage.

'I'm hungry, Mummy', Chris complained. 'Can I have a pakora?'

'No dear. You might get ill. Daddy is getting some drinks.'

Daddy came back and slammed the carriage door. She had a dim memory of opening bottles of something fizzy, but it couldn't be 7UP, that treat of their later childhood, because she was sure that hadn't come to India yet. It was the conversation which she remembered, Dad looking grave as the train started, with a jolt and a long hoot to warn pedestrians on the track ahead. He spoke seriously and included Rachel as a now nearly grown-up person. 'Gandhi has been assassinated.'

'What's ass ... what's that?' she asked, always interested in a new word.

'It means he's been killed, shot dead.'

Rachel knew that Gandhi was a great and good man. She had seen pictures of him in his dhoti or seated at a spinning wheel, his round glasses perched on his nose. She knew that the new Indian flag had a spinning wheel on it because of Gandhi. Dad had told her about it.

'Why?' she asked. But her parents were talking quietly, seriously to each other. He was saying how bad it was and what would happen now?

'What year was that?' Rachel thought coming back to the present. Was it 1947? 1948? She should look it up. She suddenly wanted to know. Perhaps Wikipedia would have an entry. Of course, she thought as she went upstairs to open her laptop, Gandhi, Gandhi-ji as they called him affectionately in India, the man died, but his ideas of non-violent resistance lived on, were taken up by the American Civil Rights Movement and in the Peace Movement here in the old centre of colonial power.

Strange, how that child on the Indian train became the woman who thirty years later in the 1970s and 1980s was taking part in acts of civil disobedience and training women's groups in non-violent resistance. Sitting in front of the gates at the Cruise Missile base in Greenham Common was surprisingly connected to the Indian railway system in her life. Of course, she'd never thought of that connection when she had been sitting on the cold tarmac in front of Yellow Gate in Greenham waiting to be moved by the Police. She had been too taken up by the present, the press of bodies, the singing 'She is like a mountain', the anxiety about being hurt by the 'Big Boys in Blue' or sent to prison and what would happen to the children then. Now she saw that one thing led to another, not just in her life but in that larger history, though how one thing led to another wasn't at all clear to her. 'Where are you from?'

There was a great deal on the net about Mahatma Gandhi (as he was known) including an article on Wikipedia. He had been killed in January 1948. She read a bit on the influence of his ideas about non-violent resistance to authority. Martin Luther King, Nelson Mandela. Steve Biko, John Lennon, even Obama, all had been influenced by him. Interesting, Rachel thought, as she trawled through the sites, that the Peace Movement doesn't get a mention anywhere. Of course, the British Peace Movement drew much of its patterns of protest from the American Civil Rights movement, rather than directly from Gandhi, but still why has that movement disappeared so completely from the historical records? And yet, at the time, we were huge. Wikipedia, after all, that great resource of factfinders, never even mentioned it in their articles on peace movements. Where are we now, those thousands of women who embraced the Greenham Common missile base in ...? Heavens! What year was that – 1982?

She found another site, and saw that she was wrong about the Indian flag. The Gandhian spinning wheel in the middle of the three stripes had been the flag of the Indian National Congress Party, which was adapted when India gained its independence but with the spinning wheel replaced by a chakra which – she read – represented dharma or the rule of law. However, there was another Gandhian connection which she had forgotten. The Indian flag had by law to be made of khadi cotton or silk, the Gandhian cloth, the sign of simple living, self-sufficiency and independence from the West.

Perhaps the circle on the Indian flag should be the wheel of a train. After all, she found as she looked at the references to various scholarly articles which came up on Google Scholar, the railways had been thought to be the great force for modernisation by the nineteenth-century British rulers of India. She found another article; this one was about the railway colonies, the housing which the railway companies provided for the workers. She thought of the railway village laid out neatly behind the station in Madurai, which she had once visited. The houses were laid out in rows and brick-built, not like the higgledy-piggledy mud and palm-leaf huts round the compound with the drying cow pats on the wall. But the brick of the neat houses was worn, the paint peeling and there was just the same smell in the street, the familiar cows nosing in the rubbish. It was where the Anglo-Indians lived. It was the Anglo-Indians who worked on the railways. According to this article she had found, these railway villages were meant to bring the civilising virtues of domesticity to the colonial peoples. Ironic really. What's the connection between railways and having a tidy house? Travel and home? It was a bitter colonial joke. Of course, we Brits always thought we were best at everything including housework, but most of those who thought so never did an hour of housework in their lives.

Suddenly Rachel remembered Louise, who had for a short time come to help out with childminding. Louise had been one of the various childminders who passed though Rachel's early life in lieu of an ayah. She was an Anglo-Indian from the railway colony. She wore her dark hair neatly in a bun and always wore a dark-blue dress, never a sari. She was serious, quiet, everything a lady should be. She had tried in her gentle way to suggest that Rachel and Chris should sit down sometimes and not play outside in the dust under the kundamani tree.

Now as Rachel thought about Louise she realised that, as an Anglo-Indian, she must have been caught between the Indian and British parts of her inheritance. In the late 1940s and early 1950s, those early days of Indian independence, what was the place of the Anglo-Indian? The new India was doubtful about these mixed-race descendants of the Raj. Britain was not welcoming to those who decided to go 'home' to the Motherland they had never seen. Some of those women who had been on the boat going back to England after the war were perhaps Anglo-Indian women who were leaving the country of their birth for a colder place.

Rachel switched off the computer and looked out of her window for a moment remembering that first voyage 'home' when she had been – what? – five or six? Years later Mum had told her it had been a nightmare. It was an old P and O boat which had been converted into a troop ship and in 1946 had still not been converted back again. There were so many people – women especially – wanting to get back to England as soon as the war ended that they just packed them in. 'Fourteen people, including children, sleeping in a cabin designed for two,' Mum had said. 'And it took nearly a month. You all had amoebic dysentery and Jane was so ill we thought she would die.'

'It must have been a very big cabin for two', Rachel had said. She had a dim memory of rows of bunks, a strange woman with long dark hair shouting at her from the top level.

'Lots of the women really did not know what they were going back to,' Mum had said. 'I often wondered about them. Caught between two worlds.'

'Like you,' Rachel thought, but did not say. She could not disentangle that memory from later journeys. Her chief feeling about those long sea voyages between India and 'home' was the sense of the child's delight at being able to roam the ship, especially in rough weather when most of the adults were in their cabins being sick. She and Chris had run about the deck and even gone into the dining room by themselves where all the table were roped off at one end and the heaving floor pushed all the furniture against the rope on the upswing of the wave so it looked as if everything might break loose and crash across the room.

Once, in a storm in the Bay of Biscay, she and Chris were on the stairs between their cabin and the upper deck, when they met a man staggering under a huge block of ice roped to his back. He must have been carrying it from the hold up to the kitchens. No fridges in those days. As Rachel and Chris came down the stairs, the ship dropped beneath them, down, down, and then staggered and began to rise, but the man staggered too and the block of ice slipped and crashed onto the floor. Small chips of ice flew up. One hit her on the knee.

Chris was frightened. 'The ship might sink!' she sobbed. 'It's an iceberg.'

'Let's go back to find Mummy,' Rachel said holding Chris's hand down the stairs. She knew the story about the Titanic but she knew this was not an iceberg and she felt the thrill and throb of the boat as if it were some great beast carrying them to safety. Like Jonah in the whale, perhaps. In old age the throb of an engine – felt, rather than heard, in the bowels of a ship – still gave her a sense of delight.

Of course, now the journey to India could be done in ten or eleven hours, rather than three or four weeks. People thought nothing of going there for a week's holiday. Travel meant something quite different. Kids set off on gap years, saying they didn't know where they would land up but they all had mobile phones and credit cards and parents who would rescue them if they got into difficulties – at least the kind of young people who went on gap years did.

But those weren't the only travellers who set off not knowing quite where they were going. They set off now not in the great ocean liners of Rachel's youth but in the belly of planes, hidden in the backs of lorries, or in tiny unseaworthy boats which more often than not sank before they reached the other side. Rachel looked at the clock and realised she would be late to meet her friend, Mary, if she did not set off now.

Then you shall declare before the Lord your God: 'My father was a wandering Aramean', Rachel said – but only to herself. They would certainly lock her up as a mad old woman if she started going around quoting bits of the Bible out loud on her suburban street. Deuteronomy, wasn't it? Abraham. Big Daddy to all of them – Jews, Christians, Muslims.

I suppose,' Rachel thought, 'that Dad was a bit of an Abraham figure. He went out to a strange land, leaving everything behind. Of course, he did know where he was going. Or did he? Those trunks packed with all the tropical kit, much of it never needed, like the topee he never wore. Perhaps he and Mum went out in the 1930s to a country already disappearing. He told me once that the list given him by the Church for what he would need to take out to India on their first term in 1936 had included 'Black evening socks, six pairs', suitable wear for all those colonial dinner parties which he and Mum never attended. What were 'evening socks'? she wondered. Anyway, moth got them all in the end.

And Abraham had been prepared to sacrifice his child when he thought it was God's will.

The *Big Issue* seller outside Boots, a Roma from somewhere in Eastern Europe, greeted her as he always did. She was one of his regulars. He had little English and today he looked cold but someone had given him a hot drink in a polystyrene cup which he was cradling.

WHERE ARE YOU FROM?

Mary was waiting for her outside the local caff. Of course, she wouldn't go in on her own. 'Sorry to be late,' said Rachel. 'Just off the train. I'm having a soup. Do you want something?' She carried the food and coffees to a table in the corner. 'How you doing?'

'Landlord still refusing to do anything about the leak,' said Mary. Mary was her English name. 'And I got another death threat.' She pulled out an airmail envelope with strange-looking stamps in the corner. Rachel read the letter as she ate, then said, 'We must take it to the Solicitor. I'll take a copy and give it back to you at the meeting if you like. Have you heard anything?'

'No,' Mary drank her coffee. 'They keep asking me why I don't have any papers as though…' she broke off. 'Did you see that thing in the paper about bogus asylum seekers?'

'Yes,' said Rachel. 'It's awful. People are just told lies. I am sorry. We just have to keep on. I know they keep saying it is safe for you to go back now but that letter shows it isn't. Try not to worry.'

They drank their coffee in silence for a moment. The place was filling up, the noise of other conversations rose around them. 'Do you want me to come round when you ring the landlord?'

'No, I'll be fine. Lady at the bus stop asked me where I came from,' said Mary. 'I think she was kind but, you know.'

'I know. It's okay for me. I am white but when people say that to you they mean "Go home" like those awful Home Office vans they sent round London. As though home was … Well. We've got a meeting of the campaign group on Sunday, haven't we?'

'Yes. After church. Ooh! Is that the time? I must go.'

'Don't ask where I'm from. Ask where I'm going,' said Rachel.

'Well. I am going to catch a bus. I'm late already.' Mary was on her way to the project where she volunteered.

'Great to see you,' Rachel said as she got up and gave her friend a hug. 'Love the coat.'

'Didsbury Oxfam,' said Mary, smoothing the fabric with her hand. 'Good, isn't it? See you Sunday.'

'Sunday,' said Rachel. 'I've got some shopping to do and then I must go home and do some emails.' She collected her shopping bag and followed Mary out into the street. 'Here we have no abiding city.' It was one of Dad's favourite Bible sayings but that didn't seem much help now and, of course, he meant something different, somewhere different.

There were all those Old Testament nomads, of course, who wandered about in the desert, and the forty years for the Children of Israel, and Paul, always on his missionary journeys that you had to make maps of in RE at school. Nobody did that at school now, of course. Paul had been on the move all the time, tramping along on the Roman roads, no doubt talking and arguing with Luke or whoever, about that other man who had tramped the roads with a gaggle of followers. And all those people on the move now. The Roma *Big Issue* seller, Mary, the children escaping Afghanistan.

Foxes have dens. Like that fox in the back garden the other night. Birds of the air have nests. But still ... they have nowhere to lay their heads.

She went into the Co-op to buy something for tea.

EDINBURGH AGAIN

Rachel's Journal
12 April 2010
Amy and I went out on Saturday and walked up above Dovestones.
The reservoir was brimming, a few sailing boats on the water catching
the wind which was gusting up the valley. It was blowing on the top,
too. We walked along the scarp looking down onto the valley and
across to the other side, the war memorial, the grey fall of rock. It
was still quite wintry, grey stones and the grass bleached of colour but
wonderfully clear and the paths not too boggy. Every time we come up
here it is different. We were remembering the day we came up in heavy
snow last year. Glad I can still do it, even though I'm slower.

There was an article in the paper the other day about cities within
sight of mountains. There were Salzburg, Venice, and Edinburgh, of
course, with the Pentland Hills and its own Arthur's Seat. But also
Manchester, which pleased me. I love it that I can live in the city and
get up into the hills or walk in the Country Park out of my door.

Amy was suggesting I went with her to Edinburgh when she
goes up for a meeting. Perhaps I'll go. Maybe I can climb Arthur's
Seat, get a bird's eye view of the city, look across to 'the Kingdom
of Fife', which always sounded so magical to me as a child, like
the Kingdom of Heaven, I suppose. But it was India we wanted to
see from the top. That was the magical place for us – the plains far
below us, mist rising as we looked down from the hills.

'I am going up to Edinburgh for a couple of days.' Rachel was on
the phone to Hannah.

'Going away again?'

'Well, Amy is going up for a meeting so she offered to drive me.
I'm revisiting my past, you know.'

'Ah! Remind me.'

'Well, I was born in Edinburgh.'

'I thought you were born in India.'

'No. I should have been but my Dad had been in an accident not long after they got to India so eventually, after various doctors failed to patch him up, they sent him back to Edinburgh. So I was born there, They took me back to India when I was three months old and Dad was off crutches.'

'So, you won't remember it.'

'Oh! But I do. We lived there on furlough twice.'

'Furlough?'

Of course, another Hobson-Jobson word, Rachel thought. 'It's what they called their times back home in England – well – Scotland, though they always said England.'

'You can tell me all about it when you get back. The ME is bad today so I don't have a lot of energy. Sorry.'

'Poor you!' said Rachel. 'I'll be in touch.' Twenty years ago, she had been off work for months with something which might have been ME or post-viral fatigue and knew how some days it could make even speaking on the phone an effort. Hannah had her good days and her bad ones. She would go to see her when she got back.

She went to put a few things into her overnight bag. It must have been hard for Dad and Mum, his accident so soon after they got to India. Did they think about giving up? Of course, she had known about the accident and the compensation piano and the funny scar on Dad's foot but she had never thought about it properly before. How different everything would have been if … but, no, Dad always said it was when he really learned Tamil, those months of inactivity.

She put a warm top into her overnight bag. It was April, but there was a chill in the air. Her abiding memory of Edinburgh was of feeling cold. The kitchen was the only room that ever got warm in that Church of Scotland house where they had stayed for two furloughs, the first when Rachel was six, going on seven; the second when she was twelve. They mostly lived in that kitchen with the washing on the racks overhead; though on Sundays they went into the front room with its heavy furniture, its battered piano and the picture of cows that frightened Chris.

Dad had taught her how to light a fire in the grate there, rolling newspaper into little circles and balancing a few twigs and small bits of coal on top, while you lit the match and hoped it would catch, so that you could put on bigger lumps of coal. Then he would hold a newspaper over the front of the grate to create a draught saying, 'Don't *you* do this.' Once the paper had caught fire and blazed up. He dropped it on the dark green tiles of the hearth and beat out the flames with the poker. It was exciting but terrifying. That was their second time in the house. It must have been 1951. Rachel got quite good at lighting fires and helping with the little ones, but once after washing up she was carrying an uneven pile of plates which slipped out of her hands and smashed to pieces on the kitchen floor. Those plates had been a strange assortment of shapes and sizes but they were all there was and Rachel burst into tears. 'We'll have to tell the Church,' Mum said. The plates belonged to the Church. Everything in the house, except their clothes, belonged to the Church. When Dad came home he said, 'It was an accident. Everyone has accidents,' and Rachel felt better.

Oh! those Edinburgh furlough houses, Rachel thought to herself as she zipped up her bag. It would be strange to see it again, that Morningside house. Now she realised the neighbours probably thought it lowered the tone of the street with its shabby curtains, the untidy garden and all the going and coming of missionary families with their assorted children. The house itself, all that heavy old furniture, the worn lino in the kitchen, the dark paint, all were the relics of the pious souls who had left their house to the Church when they died. It always smelled damp and fusty, a bit like the Kodai houses when you first arrived in the hills but somehow the smell there never went away.

'I think it was hard for my Mum,' she said to Amy as they drove up the motorway next morning, 'especially that first furlough just after the war. All her family had died or moved away from Edinburgh and she had three small children who were ill the whole time. We arrived from India with amoebic dysentery and then we all got measles and whooping cough. Jane was so ill they thought she would die. Everyone said it was 'verra warm' that autumn, but we were cold all the time.'

'Well, of course, you'd come from India.'

'Yes and coal was rationed. Households were expected to build up their stocks in summer to last through the winter. But we hadn't been there in the summer and that winter, the winter of 1946 to 47, was terrible. Lots of people died. They said it was the coldest for three centuries. Then Mum had all the managing the household and the washing. The washing!'

Mum was used to having the dhobi come every week to take the dirty clothes and wash them in the river, bashing them clean on the rocks and then spreading them out in the fierce sun to dry. In Edinburgh, she did the washing in the basement. Rachel remembered the basement clearly. You had to go down the steep stone stairs where she had once fallen and cut her chin. It bled and bled. There was a sink which Rachel realized now must have been very low for Mum because it was a good height for Rachel who sometimes tried to 'help' her mother, swishing the clothes round in the sink, getting herself and the floor soaking and then shouting to Chris to 'Come and see!' as Mum fed the wet clothes through the mangle. They thought it was magic the way the clothes went in wet and then ballooned out at the end before landing all flat in the other sink. It didn't feel like magic to Mum as she wrestled to turn the heavy handle. Sometimes the wet sheets and towels could be hung on the line in the back garden, a patch of scrubby grass. More often the wet clothes were put onto the rack in the kitchen where they added to the damp in the air.

'Of course,' Rachel said, 'We all wore clothes for much longer then and nobody had washing machines.'

'When did you get your first machine?'

'We bought a second-hand twin-tub just after Anne was born. Do you remember them? Transformed my nappy washing.'

'Yes, we got a twin tub, but then I'm young enough to have used disposable nappies.'

'Lucky you!'

They drove in silence as Rachel remembered. It was such a great day when she and Peter had bought that twin-tub from the warehouse in Whalley Range not long after Annie was born. Oh those nappies! After you had soaked them overnight in a bucket of – what was that stuff called? – you put them in the washer and then hauled the wet nappies and clothes out of the wash tub with those big wooden tongs, and put them through the mangle into the rinse tub. Then at the end you turned the mangle over the sink and put the rinsed clothes through it, hanging them up on the pulley in the kitchen. Rachel somehow always ended with the floor awash with soapy water, but it was hugely better than the old basement in Edinburgh. Still, a long way from the automatic she had now.

Peter's Auntie Mu had come back from church one Sunday in the 1970s furious because the minister had preached a sermon denouncing the washing machine as the work of the devil! 'He never lifts a finger in the house!' she snorted. 'Wouldn't know how to wash a pair of socks or even a cup, if he had to.' Washing, apparently, was part of the labour of Eve's daughters. A punishment for sin. Women's work!

'Mum and Auntie May and all the women I knew did their washing on a Monday so you could have cold meat from the Sunday joint,' Rachel said.

'Yes, of course. Then you put the remains of the cold meat though the mincer for shepherd's pie on Tuesday.' They both laughed.

'But,' Rachel said, 'I did the same in the early 1970s when the girls were little. Hard to believe now.' Yes, she thought, looking out unseeing at the countryside, it was always roast on Sunday, cold meat on Monday, mince on Tuesday and so on, through to 'fish on Fridays'. Everyone had fish on Fridays, though this had no liturgical significance for me, though perhaps it did for Auntie May. How strange it seems now. But that was the order of things! And had been since the Victorian era. They were the rituals of domesticity, the round of washing and cleaning, of periods and childbirth, not the linear history of great battles and intellectual triumphs. She and Amy had read Julia Kristeva's essay *Women's Time* when they had taught the Women's Studies MA together. They knew about the circularity of women's work.

'Does anybody do Sunday dinner now?' she said.

'Yes. I do, occasionally,' Amy laughed.

Morningside, symbol of Edinburgh posh, seemed a more mixed place as they drove through. The mansions round the foot of the Braid Hills, the grey-stone houses with their red sandstone surrounds and the old terraces were solidly respectable but some of the shops on Morningside Road looked shabby and neglected. The hills, though, were the same, both the distant Pentlands and the city roads which swept up and down as they always had, though now they seemed narrower, steeper and without the trams which had been the delight of Rachel and Chris's life. The Mound was the best where the trams clanked and rattled at terrifying speeds down the bend towards Princes Street, but even the swoop on Morningside Road generated a thrilling speed and clatter.

They parked the car and walked along the road, her road, the road whose every lamp post and corner she remembered, except that she didn't. It was narrower, more cramped, the road was steeper and the bend where she had come off her bike and gone into the lamp post was sharper. She still had the scar on her knee. Like clothes bought 'to be grown into' the bikes she and Chris were given that year were full-size with wooden blocks on the pedals. Hers was still big for her at university.

They walked past number 21. It was as she remembered it, a two-storey terrace house of grey stone but it had shrunk and the front garden was tiny. The Church of Scotland had sold off all its furlough houses. There was no call for them now. Someone lived there all the time, the someone who had painted the front door green, put pots of geraniums in the front garden and hung bright curtains. She didn't knock at the door but walked past slowly trying to see into the room without peering too obviously.

It was in the second furlough they lived here when she was twelve that Rachel had spent so much time in that dark front room. It was always cold. Even lighting the fire on Sundays never warmed it. Nothing had changed in the five years since their last furlough. The old mottled-brown piano was still in the front room, but now Rachel could play it. For years, she had been having lessons in Kodai with Miss Ruth.

'Perhaps we could get it tuned,' said Dad, playing a few chords and making a face.

'Yes, please, Daddy,' said Rachel, so the piano tuner came and Rachel played the piano whenever she could. It was summer, but she would put on her coat and sit on the wobbly piano stool and she would play.

When Rachel had gone to say goodbye, Miss Ruth had given her a yellow-covered book with 'Sonatas by Clementi' in it. Rachel had cried because she loved Miss Ruth even though she was old and strict and wore her hair in a bun. And she cried because she didn't want to leave Kodai and go back to school in England. Miss Ruth told her, 'You can play the piano and, when you do, you can remember Kodai and all your friends.' The sonatas were hard but Rachel loved them. Playing a whole sonata felt grown up.

Besides, playing the piano was about the only thing Rachel could do. Even though she had been going to school for years, she found now that she had been taught nothing that mattered. She read all the time, of course, but those books didn't count, and she knew lots of outdoors games like Kick-the-can, Beckon, Sardines (you could play that inside too, of course), how to make a den and how to hide in the bushes so quietly that it took a long time for anyone to find you. She could climb trees and walk miles through the sholas and she could row a boat, but none of those things counted now. There were no climbing trees or sholas or boats in Edinburgh.

'Rachel and Christine are going to boarding school next term but they are so far behind children here, especially Rachel. Luckily, I have found a school that's agreed to take Christine just for this term. And they have said Rachel can go in the afternoons and we are looking to various friends and people we know to give her coaching in the mornings,' Mum had explained to Mrs Johnston-next-door, who had come in for a cup of tea.

Coaching turned out to be going to different people's houses to have lessons all on your own. Chris and Jane could go to school. Jane had just started and Mum used to walk to school with her and Chris every morning, holding Jim's hand. He could walk quite well now. But Chris didn't like going to that school.

'I wish I was you,' she said to Rachel.

'You wouldn't like coaching,' said Rachel, but she secretly did like going out on her own to learn French, which was all about Madame Sourie and her family of mice, or Latin, which was learning by heart. Miss Macdonald who coached her for Latin was ill and lay in bed while Rachel sat on a low chair by the bed and chanted '*amo, amas, amat, amamus, amatis, amant*', out of a purple book called *Kennedy's Latin Grammar*. It had been Miss Macdonald's book when she was at school but she said, 'Latin has not changed very much since I and your Mummy and Daddy were young, even though that was a long time ago.'

She went on the bus to Mrs Brown's to do 'Maths'. Maths was

not just arithmetic but all sorts of other things which Rachel used to get into a muddle about. Mrs Brown lived in Colinton and going there on the bus was the best thing about coaching. Rachel went on the upstairs of the bus as it went up and up until you could see the green line of the Pentland hills where they sometimes used to go hiking when Daddy was at home.

'It's not called hiking in England,' Mum said, 'it's called walking.'

'This is Scotland,' said Rachel, 'not England.'

'Well, it's not called hiking in Scotland either. Hiking is American.'

Mrs Brown gave her 'homework' to do. They didn't have homework in Kodai. Rachel sat at the kitchen table when she got back and tried to work out the maths until it was time to go to school or help with the washing up or making beds.

In the afternoons, she had to go to school. Everyone else went there all day and the teachers sometimes forgot that Rachel was there and sometimes forgot she hadn't been there in the mornings. You had to have uniforms for that school. Because it was summer, uniform was blue and white striped dresses and navy-blue cardigans and blazers. Mrs Johnston had given Mum some old school dresses from her girls, which fitted Chris and Jane, but Rachel didn't have any uniform.

'The Head Mistress has said you don't need it because you are only going in the afternoons for a term.'

'But, Mummy, all the other girls have it.'

'It's expensive.'

'Please! Please! Please!' said Rachel.

In the end Mum got her a navy-blue cardigan and Rachel pulled it down as far as it would go to hide her dress, which was not blue and white stripes.

They did Science at school. Rachel wrote in her best writing in her Science notebook:

'There are three forms of heating: convection, conduction and radiation.' She learned all about convection but she missed conduction and radiation because they were in the morning. One day the teacher, who was called Miss Lewis, said they would have a test. Rachel had never done a test before. You had to sit quietly and write down your name and the date at the top of a bit of paper.

Then the teacher read out questions and you had to write down the answers without talking. But Rachel did not understand all the questions and when it came to radiation she put up her hand and said 'Please, Miss Lewes, I didn't do radiation or conduction. I only did convection.' Miss Lewes said, 'Well do the best you can, Rachel.' But Rachel wasn't there when the tests were given back so she never knew about radiation.

The best thing at school was poetry. They all learned 'The king sat in Dunfermline toon, drinking the blud red wine.' Rachel learned it all by heart and loved to say it to herself making all the Scottish words roll round her mouth. The other girls spoke like that but they laughed at the way Rachel spoke.

'You're a Yank,' they said to Rachel. 'Talk yankee to us.'

'I am not. I am Scottish. I was born in Edinburgh,' she said.

'Why do you talk like that, then?'

'Because I went to an American school.'

'But you said you were from India.'

'It was an American school in India.'

They laughed and said, 'Liar! Liar! pants on fire', and 'Got her school dress in India,' but mostly they took no notice of her.

At the end of school Rachel walked back with Chris and Jane. Mummy said they could walk back on their own, but Rachel had to hold Jane's hand. The worst thing was the gangs of George Watson boys in their purple blazers. Rachel though they were a bit like the buffalos round the lake in Kodai. You never knew quite what they would do. But Rachel had to look after Chris and Jane now, so she tried to walk along without taking any notice, holding Jane's hand. Sometimes Mum came with Jim to the top of their road to meet them.

'He has recovered wonderfully from the polio, hasn't he?' said Auntie Dot, Mum's friend, when they visited her house in Morningside.

'Yes,' said Mum. 'It is amazing. A miracle. The doctors here have said he doesn't have to be strapped on the board anymore. He is still meant to do exercises with his feet but I am afraid they often get neglected.'

'We'll show you,' said Rachel and Chris and they took off their shoes and socks and showed how Jim had to walk on the sides of his feet holding a little ball in his toes. Then Jim did it and everyone clapped him.

When summer holidays came, Dad had to go back to India and the rest of them went to stay with Auntie May in Huyton for a few weeks while she and Mum got everything ready for Rachel and Chris to go to their new school, which was near London and was called Walthamstow Hall. Rachel worried that all the other girls would call her a yank and know about maths and radiation. But Mum said to her, 'You know, I was sent home to go to school when I was seven. You are twelve now. Auntie May will be your guardian and you must look after Chris and be helpful to Auntie May while we are out in India.'

They had stayed with Auntie May before, when James was born. But then Auntie May lived in a different house with John and Wendy, the dog. Daddy had told Rachel and Chris that John had gone to be with Jesus. All that was a long time ago, when Rachel was seven and Chris was five. Now Rachel and Chris were 'great big girls', as Auntie May said. Her new house was a squash for them all but it was not for long – just while they got everything ready for the new school.

Rachel was surprised to find she had tears in her eyes and had been standing looking at the house for far too long. 'Coming?' said Amy. 'Let's find something to eat.'

INTERLUDE
(1951–2)

PREPARATIONS

There were so many clothes to be bought for the new school. Mummy was going through the list: 'one n-- brown pullover with yellow-stripe, one brown school skirt, two white lining knickers, two n-- brown knickers, two vests, two liberty bodices ...'

'What's a liberty bodice?'

'What's the difference between ordinary brown and n-- brown?'

Mummy did not answer but started doing sums with a pencil on the back of the long brown envelope (was it n-- brown?) in which the list had come.

'We didn't have lists for our school in India,' Christine said. 'Did we, Mummy?'

Mummy stopped and thought for a moment. 'I think they said you had to have a good strong pair of shoes. Oh! And a canteen, one of those army surplus tin water bottle things with a khaki cover to take on hikes.'

'But we never had one of those.'

'No. But you always had good shoes, bought from Bata.'

She went on looking at the list, '... n-- brown gabardine, n-- brown velour hat, panama hat.'

'Hats! Do we have to wear hats?'

'Yes. You are big girls now.'

'But, what for?'

'Well, going out, to church, I suppose.'

'You never made us wear topees.'

'Yes, but it is different in England.'

Some of the things on the list had to be bought in a very expensive shop in London called Peter Robinson but some could be bought in Liverpool. They all had to go on the train from Huyton station, Mummy and Rachel and Chris and Jane and James and Auntie May. They got the train from Huyton station to Liverpool

Lime Street. Rachel was used to England now. She no longer looked for the lime sellers in the station, where the trains sent steam up towards the black glass roof and people walked past without looking at you. But it still felt strange to be in a station where there was no one sleeping on the floor, no shouting, no one selling chai, no smells of cooking or bustle.

They went to a huge shop with a dark brown floor and counters and lots of white ladies behind the counters. People in the shops in England were all white. Everyone was white. Even in the street there were no Indian women in red and orange saris squatting by the road breaking stones or walking in long lines with baskets of earth on their heads. Instead there were white men with shovels and spades. Everyone was dressed in grey or black or brown. The sky was grey.

The shop was called Lewis's and they were going to buy knickers and liberty bodices, which turned out to be a funny kind of vests with stripes on them and dangling down bits. You had to wear so many clothes here.

'The girls will need pyjamas,' Mummy said to Auntie May, looking at the list.

'I never had a pair of pyjamas bought in a shop,' Chris said to the lady behind the counter. 'We had American cast-offs.'

'Gracious! What a thing to say!' said Auntie May giving her a sharp push. 'Don't talk like that.'

'Why not?' said Chris. It was true and she and Rachel knew they should always speak the truth. When they were in India the clothes that came in parcels from America were always exciting. Most of their clothes had been made by the tailor who would come now and then and sit on the veranda. They loved him coming, Rachel and Chris. They would squat beside him on the cool concrete floor of the back veranda as he sat cross legged, turning the handle of the sewing machine, making skirts and tops like magic. But some of their best clothes came out of the parcels, what Mummy called 'American cast-offs'. Rachel loved them. Mummy did too. She had once had a dress she specially liked. She said it was 'new look' and it was white with a big twirly skirt. It had bunches of pink and blue flowers on it and pink twisty lines which made words.

PREPARATIONS

'Ap-ril show-ers bring May flow-ers,' Rachel read out.

'Goodness!' said Mummy,' I hadn't realised they were words. Oh dear! I can't wear it now.' Rachel was sad. She liked the dress. It was pretty and said something about May. Auntie May was Mummy's sister, like Chris and she were sisters. Rachel tried to think of Auntie May and Mummy as little girls but she couldn't.

In England people didn't get parcels from America. There were no tailors who came and sat on the veranda with their sewing machines, there were no verandas. Here in England everything was different.

'Why do we have to have two of everything, Mummy?'

'One to wear and one for the wash. Yes, see here on the list. "Wash bag". You will wear your vests and socks and knickers one week and then you will have to put them in the wash bag and put on clean ones. I expect you will do that on bath night.'

'Are there dhobis in England?' Rachel had looked for them on the train as they went over a river, but there were none.

'Well, they are not called dhobis and they don't wash clothes in the river. The clothes wouldn't get very clean and they would never get dry on the rocks here. It rains too much,' and she laughed.

'I don't like the rain here,' said Chris.

'What's the matter with the child?' said Auntie May. 'Where's your Irish blood? It rains all the time on the west coast of Ireland where your Mummy comes from.'

'But it's soft rain,' said Mummy. 'Soft.' And she gave Chris a little smile.

'All items of clothing must be clearly labelled with Christian name and surname. We advise Cash's labels,' Mummy read out when they were back at Auntie May's with the parcels. 'I ordered them last month and they came yesterday. Well named they are – cash! Let's see.'

Cash's labels came in a little flat tube. Inside was a long white ribbon with your name on it in red letters. Chris's said Christine Newby and Rachel's said Rachel Newby. It was magic. But sewing them on was not. 'You are old enough to help your Mother and me,' Auntie May said to Rachel. The thread tied itself in knots. The material was tough, especially the n-- brown knickers which were thick wool. The red letters got smeared with blood. It was not like darning. Darning was fun. You held the mushroom under the sock and made a criss-cross pattern with the thread. At Kodai on Friday nights the girls would all sit on the floor in the big upstairs room and do darning together. Miss Jenner read out loud stories about brave American missionaries and women like Madame Chiang Kai-shek, who was Chinese.

'I don't want to go to school and wear liberty bodices and n-- brown knickers,' said Chris.

'I went to that school when I was a little girl,' said Mummy, 'and I know you will like it. It was like a home to me.'

'Can't I go back to India with you and Jane and Jim, please, please, Mummy.'

But Mummy looked sad and said, 'No darling. You are going to stay here and go to school and be a big girl, so that when we come back again we can be so proud of you.'

'When will you come back, Mummy?'

'Well. It will be five years. Perhaps when Jane is as big as you are now, we will come back and she can go to school with you. But I will write to you every week and you can write to me. You will go to school and Auntie May will look after you in the holidays and you can go to Granny's sometimes. You will like that won't you?'

She looked at Rachel. 'You will have to be a big girl and help to look after Chris when I am gone. Write to me every week and tell me how she is and how you are.'

'Yes, Mummy.'

That night in bed Chris cried and cried. Mummy came in and sat on the bed. 'Do you have a pain, Chris, dear?'

'Yes.'

'Where is it? Is it a tummy pain?'

'I don't know.'

'Can I get you something to make it better?'

'Take me back to India,' she sobbed. 'Take me back to India with you.'

◆

PREPARATIONS

'Home for the holidays, is it?' The cheerful ticket man asked as he opened the train compartment door. It was one of those trains with a corridor. 'Where are you off to then, you two?' Rachel handed him the little book of tickets which had been entrusted to her by Miss Green. Miss Green was the art teacher and she had come with Rachel and Chris to Charing Cross station to set them on their way.

'Do you have everything, Rachel? Tickets? Money? Packed lunch?'

'Yes, Miss Green.'

'Who is meeting you in Liverpool?'

'Auntie May.'

'And are you sure she knows which train you are on?'

'Yes, Miss Green. I wrote to her and told her.'

Rachel was a veteran now of these journeys – an experienced thirteen-year-old who knew all about lost tickets and meeting people at stations. 'Under the clock at Charing Cross', or 'By the WHSmith's on Lime Street Station'.

'Well, you are going it!' the ticket man said, looking at the little green booklet with bits of paper stapled into it which they had instead of the usual tickets. They were going first to Liverpool then to Newcastle then back again, trundling round Britain like a pair of misdirected parcels. 'Travellers, aren't you?'

'Yes,' Rachel said primly. 'We are.'

Once he had gone they settled down to enjoy the train. They always liked the long journeys up north, unless some misguided adult decided to intervene to ask about these two little girls travelling on their own. Usually no one bothered. Today they had a carriage to themselves. The n-- brown gabardines were slung on the luggage rack overhead, the hated velour hats squashed flat under them. They had a small bag each. Most of their things were in the cabin trunk, the battered old friend which went to and fro every holiday, covered with layers of old labels which were stuck on and showed through the newer ones: Bombay, Colombo, Southampton, London, Madras, Tilbury, London, Newcastle, Edinburgh, Liverpool.

They looked out of the window at the impossibly green countryside. England had its colours, too and they were accustomed now to them, the grey skies, the fields so unlike the parched brown landscape of South India. The telegraph wires swooped and dipped. The train soothed with its clickety click, clickety click. They ate their packed lunch. School sandwiches were always the same but at least they had included some bread and jam ones, deliciously soggy, the red seeping into the white in a chewy sweetness. Rachel read her book. Chris sat looking out of the window. They did not speak.

Early photographs of 'Chris' (Alison, on the left in both pictures) and 'Rachel' (me, on the right). The picture with Mum and Dad, on the front steps of our Kodai house, is from 1942, and the second one a year or two later.

Further early pictures of me, top left, and Alison, top right. The lower image, from around 1948, sees us balanced on the edge of something precarious either side of 'James' (John) and 'Jane' (Janet).

Punting with Dad on Lake Kodai, 1946.

Kodai Lake, and the view from St Peter's Church, Kodaikanal.

My school, Walthamstow Hall, in Kent, England, 1948.

Mum's Irish aunts – the 'Chestnut sisters' – at their home in Tralee, Ireland; Dad at a formal event in the 1950s, as Bishop of Madurai and Ramnad.

Mum gardening, probably in the 1950s; Dad on a train; together in retirement during the 1980s.

My sister (left) and me on the only hill walk we did together as adults (2002/3?). A happy memory.

Mum and Dad with their children and some of their grandchildren (1996). I am third from right on second row between my two sisters with Ali ('Chris') on my right. My brother is on the left end of the row.

VI

A GOOD
EDUCATION
(2010/1951–6)

SCHOOL REUNION

Date: 2 May 2010
Subject: School; Old Girls' Reunion !!!!
Hello Sis,
Tried to ring but remembered you're away. Advice wanted. I've had a letter from Eleanor Bennett, one of the daygirls at school – in my class so you prob don't remember her. Don't know how she tracked me down. You know, I've always refused to have anything to do with school since we left. Anyway, she found my address and wrote and asked if I'd like to go to a reunion at school. It's more than fifty years since we left! Impossible to believe! You went to a 'do' at school a couple of years ago, didn't you. What do you think? Shall I go?

It's a bit weird because – did I tell you? – my old school friend, Peggy, who got in touch with me a few years ago, also wrote to me recently about school. Do you remember her? She'd disappeared off to Australia after Uni and we hadn't been in touch for years. She'd tracked me down (helped by the internet I think) on a visit to UK to see her family. She's back in Australia now but we have been emailing each other. I'm asking her advice, too.
Hope all well. I'm around so ring whenever,
Love,
R.

Date: 12 May 2010
Subject: School reunion
Dear Peggy,
Thanks for your email and your advice. Yes, Eleanor was one of those day girls who always seemed so confident about the world and who – I seem to remember – had a pony, but I might have made that up. I know she had a crush on Miss Percival the year Miss P. was our form teacher. We all had a bit of a crush on her, didn't we? We were

131

so amazed – weren't we – when she left to get married! A teacher getting married! Now I think about it, Miss P can't have been that much older than us. Remember that time she talked about being at school during the war and Eleanor asked her, 'Which war, Miss?' and she came straight back, ' The Boer War, of course.' But none of us got the joke. I think we assumed all teachers were at least a hundred.

Were any of our teachers married? I remember them all as 'spinster ladies'.

I'm not at all sure about going back. Did I tell you that Mum and Dad gave us each back some of the letters we had written to them from school? Made me remember those long Sunday afternoons with everyone sitting on their beds in silence trying to think what to say and scratching away with those awful pens! I always got blotting paper put into the ink-well on my desk in class, so my pen-nib got full of bits and made ink blotches. (The biro was a great invention, wasn't it? Not as great as the internet, of course.) When Mum gave me the letters I just stuck them away in an old trunk but I took out a couple yesterday and started to read them. Then put them all back and shut the lid.

But perhaps you're right and I should go back – lay the ghosts or defy them – or something.

Glad all's well with you. I'm attaching some photos of my holiday in the Lake District, which was lovely – we even had some sun. Don't laugh. You may remember how rare that was.

Love,

Rachel

RACHEL'S LETTER

School

12 September 1952

Dear Daddy and Mummy,

I am in the third form here. All the other girls were in the school before but there is one other girl who is new. She is called Margery but she says I can call her Peggy and we sit together because we are new. We have to do Latin and French and Maths. I like English but I don't like games because all the other girls know how to play Larcrosse and I don't. Miss Power, the games teacher is strict. There are lots of rules here. I asked Gill who I share a cubicle with how she remembered where to be all the time but she said you get used to it. I will write out what we have to do every day.

The bell goes at 10 to 7 in the morning but you can stay in bed unless you are the water monitor. Then you have to get up and go with a big jug to the washroom and carry hot water in the jugs to pour into the basins in everyone's cubicle. The basins are on little cupboards called lockers where we keep all our clothes and things. I am water monitor next week.

7.10. The bell goes. Everyone has to get up and wash in the water brought by the water monitors, get dressed in your school uniform, and strip your bed. I am getting better at doing my tie now but first I had to get Gill to help me. It is cold. Gill and I try to stay warm in bed as long as we can but we have to be up and dressed by the 7.30 bell.

7.30. The prefect comes round to inspect you. You have to sit by your bed and be quiet and say your prayers for quarter of an hour.

7.45. The bell goes for breakfast. We all go down to the dining room. There are big tables. Chris and I are not allowed to sit together because we are sisters. Sisters are not meant to talk to each other. At breakfast, the oldest girls sit at the top near the teacher and the youngest sit at the bottom and pour out the tea. Sometimes I have to cut the bread and one of the older girls told me off for cutting it crooked. In breakfast we have the radio on for the news, which is at 8.00.

At 8.15 we go up to the dormitory to make our beds and get our books for school. We are not allowed to go up there in the day.

8.45 is school. All the day girls come in and we go to registration in our classes and then assembly when we have a hymn and some readings and Miss Burroughs sometimes talks to us.

Then we have school until dinner time.

Dinners are OK usually though sometimes we have stringy meat and sometimes we have a pudding called frogspawn which is horrible and slimy.

I don't have any more room now to tell you about things, so I will write more next Sunday.

Love,
Rachel

HOME IS WHERE

Date: 25 May 2010
Subject: School Again
Dear Peggy,

You are right. We did have a couple of married teachers. Mrs Clay, blue-rinsed Tory lady and such a great teacher. You probably won't remember but we did the American War of Independence in our first term and all I had learned about the dreadful British and brave George Washington who never told a lie was turned on its head. Mrs Clay said that it had taught me something important about history and I suppose she was right but at the time I was – well – now I think it was part of the general confusion of that first year of being 'back home', where every landmark of my life had disappeared.

You rescued me several times. I was always glad that you were a new girl at the same time, so we could share one of those double desks with the dreadful inkwells. You had had 'a good education' and knew all about Latin verbs and such-like but you didn't know your way round the school any more than I did so we could be companions in confusion!

The other married teacher, I remember now, was Mrs Moore. I think she was part-time wasn't she, when she took us for those A level English courses. Do you remember how shocked we were when she turned up to teach Hamlet wearing RED SHOES? We thought someone her age ought not to be so – I don't know what we thought but we knew that red shoes were not appropriate for OLD WOMEN. (How old was she, do you think? 50?) What prigs we were! But we did enjoy our sixth form English, didn't we? And those discussions of 'Portrait of the Artist as a Young Man' and 'Beauty' and 'Truth'.

Anyway, I am going to take your advice and go to the re-union. Wish you could be there too but it is hardly worth coming back from Queensland just for that. I'll tell you all about it.

Love, R

Date: 27 July 2010
Subject: I have survived!

Yes! I have been back to school and lived to tell the tale. It is strange, Peggy. School's exactly the same but completely different – a bit like us I suppose. There are all sorts of new classrooms and, because it no longer takes boarders and is now an expensive fee-paying school, the old dormitories are now teaching rooms and science labs (Science labs! We never had those, did we! Not suitable for young ladies.) But the old building, the entrance and red-brick front look exactly as I remember them. I almost expected Miss B. to walk out and say 'Now, gels, where are your hats?' Inside everything is now painted white instead of that dreadful 'n-- brown' paint and varnish everywhere. They still have those big fat radiators (probably worth a fortune now for 'period properties') and that sampler-thing hung by the front door with: 'Her voice was ever soft, gentle and low; An excellent thing in a woman' embroidered on it has gone. I'd like to think it was smashed by rioting pupils in the 70s but doubt it.

Our class were all having a picnic on the lawn when I arrived. Half of them looked exactly the same – but wrinkled and/or fatter – and the others were completely unrecognisable. I was the only ex-boarder; the others were all day girls. Someone asked me, 'Why do boarders never come to reunions?' And I said without thinking, 'Because they were so miserable.' But it wasn't strictly true, was it? We were miserable but we were also happy. We assumed, as children do, that this was how the world was. But talking to these 'old girls' made me realise what an odd set up it was, with a majority of very well-off local girls who had passed the eleven plus and then us, boarders, who hadn't passed any entrance exam and were mostly 'dimmies' whose parents were abroad or who came from dysfunctional families and who got our fees paid by various bodies, mostly missionary societies. You were an exception, of course. And, then Miss B. never let us forget it. Boring on about the school being founded for missionaries' children, and talking about my Dad in front of the whole school which made me and Chris feel even more like freaks.

It was divide and rule, wasn't it? Not just sisters being kept apart – we were all in separate groups, you couldn't be friends with someone from a different year and day girls didn't mix with boarders. Wendy said to me on Saturday, 'Why did none of us ever ask you to come home with us? We never thought about the kind of lives you led. I feel embarrassed now.' But I told her I thought it was structural, systemic. We were two tribes sharing the same territory and co-existing as best we could.

It is strange but I don't think I envied the day girls because they went home to their families every evening. That was just beyond imagination. I realise now how desolate we often were but that is the grown-up me mourning on behalf of my younger self – our younger selves. Did I wish that Mum or Dad or even one of the aunties had been there when I went up to get a prize at speech day? Don't think so. It wasn't until I was a university teacher and saw proud families crowding round my own graduating students that I thought, 'Well I never had anyone come to see me prance around in my graduate finery.' At the time I just accepted it – like going around different aunties in the holidays. And school was mostly so much better than the holidays. We had our friends – I only now realise how important our friendships were – and our routines and we knew what we were expected to do at every moment of the day.

I do remember your sister, of course. She was in the same class as Chris. My youngest sister, Jane, was quite 'naughty' in school, which was probably a healthy reaction. My survival strategy was to be terribly good which didn't help in the long run but got me through. You were the same, I think. Chris was the one who carried all the grief and rage into her adult life. But she wasn't naughty at school, either.

I attach photo – just to remind you!

Love, R.

Rachel's Journal

28 July

Still trying to work out my feelings after the school re-union. I did feel a bit of an oddball at this gathering, the only one who didn't live locally or at least in the home counties. (Why 'home'? I wonder, and whose?) I wandered off while the others were finishing their picnic. Wished Peggy or someone was there I could talk to. Also, as usual, I felt I wasn't dressed right among all these rather smart matronly figures but then after all I am exactly the same age! Just the only one in trousers.

I wanted to see the old 6th form common room at the top of the school where we made illegal Kendal Mint Cake and where we had those discussions about love and life and what we would do in the world. I went up to the top of the school to find the room. The stone stairs and iron-work banisters look and feel and even smell the same but the door was locked. I felt incredibly angry and rattled it. No good, of course. It wouldn't budge. I even sat down on the top step and thought that coming was all a big mistake and I would sneak off before all the meetings and speeches but I didn't. My bum got cold (those stone stairs!) and I stood up and went to find that cubicle next to the Biology lab which Peggy and I shared in Lower Sixth and which we liked so much, despite the stink of formaldehyde and always getting into trouble for reading after lights out!

Did we really have to put our lights out by 9.30 as I remember or have I made that up? Must check with Peggy. But the dormitories have all been turned into classrooms. So have all those music practice rooms, where I spent hours and hours on the piano.

I told Peggy that I survived school by being good and also – though I didn't say this to her – by being a clever clogs, even though I was no good at games. Those dreadful games periods when Peggy and I stood shivering in the cabbage patch hoping no one would throw the lacrosse ball in our direction! Chris was the one who was good at games. Oh , Chris. School did something to you and to me and to us. We stopped being able to speak to each other for years.

I must stop writing this and get on with the day.

'School took my sister from me,' Rachel thought, as she closed her journal. 'But ...' she gazed out of the window, not seeing the garden, the rooftops of the houses beyond, the high summer cloud over the city, '... school gave me friendships, passionate friendships.' She went downstairs to make a coffee. The sun broke through and she took her mug out to sit for a moment on her garden bench.

Yes, school had taken away with one hand and given with the other. It was the Saturday afternoons which sealed their – could you call it – love? It wasn't like the crushes some of the younger children had for young teachers or the older girls, but it was intimate. After the morning's study, the regular Saturday lunch of stringy meat and boiled cabbage and spotted dick, it was time to go for the compulsory walk. In the lower fourth year they had to go in groups with two members of staff. They walked in crocodile to the gate in the wall which opened into Knole Park.

'Be back here by 5.00,' the teacher would say.

Some girls groaned, walked a few yards and sat down on an old tree trunk to chat but Rachel wanted to walk. So did Peggy, so did Margaret, another girl in their class. They walked through the park, between the great grey trunks of beech tress, crunching the fallen beech mast and the drifts of bronze leaves underfoot. They saw the great house.

'It's meant to have 365 rooms, one for each day of the year,' Peggy said. 'And I think 12 staircases.'

'Have you read *Orlando*?' Rachel asked Peggy. 'It's by Virginia Woolf and it's meant to be all about Knowle House. I got it out of the Huyton library last holiday.'

'What's it like?'

'I really liked it. The man changes into a woman.'

The next year, they were allowed to walk further afield, go on their own if they promised to get back for tea. One of them bought a map. Was it Peggy? They found their way to new places, searched in the green valleys for cowslips, delicate scented yellow flowers. Bluebells in May. Mist in the woods. They walked along the Pilgrim's Way above Otford and thought of people walking to Canterbury and once they went to Toy's Hill and looked across the Weald. 'The garden of England', Kent was called. It lay all green and spread out in a faint summer haze.

Rachel discovered Wordsworth. Spots of time. Was that it? They walked out of their school lives into another time. Another space. They wore their school lace-ups and the belted brown gaberdines which were not really waterproof. When it rained the coats just got heavier with water. But, they were happy.

But then, coming back, exhausted and starving. They knew that Saturday tea was always a cold sausage roll but at least there was as much bread and jam as you could eat. Cups and cups of tea. Then in the sixth form when they had a gas-ring, using the stolen sugar from the dining hall to make those awful sweets.

Bath nights were once a week but in the sixth form Rachel and her friends sneaked extra illegal baths after their Saturday walks. Creeping up to the top floor bathroom, she and Peggy would fill the tub far above the line on the bath that showed the level you should have your bathwater. Then they would lie there, head to toe ('Your turn for the taps end!'), steaming away the week, talking and giggling in whispers in case Miss Leclerc came and found them, getting out red and happy to rub away some of the wet with the skimpy school towels, opening the door cautiously and stealing off to read novels under the bed clothes. They were never caught.

Rachel returned to the present. The Albertine above her garden bench was over its summer flush of roses and needed to be cut back, but not now. Now she wanted to walk out of her garden down to the river.

Date: 2 August 2010
Subject: School Again! Can you bear it?
Dear Peggy,

You are right about school, some of the teaching was dreadful but some of it was great. Since I went back for the re-union I have been thinking about it quite a lot and I realise how important those friendships we had at school were to me, especially yours. Of course we said hurtful things to each other at times but I think now perhaps it was those friendships that kept something important alive in me. Those long walks we used to do every Saturday when we weren't allowed to stay inside and we were peculiar and did not want to go into town and raid Woolworth's! All those passionate discussions we had in the common room and when we were listening to the news. Do you remember how angry we were about Anthony Eden and the Suez Canal debacle? I had forgotten (until you reminded me) about the debate when I proposed the motion that 'missionaries should not have children'. I don't think I really wished my own extinction or felt furious with my parents for bringing me into the world. In fact, I have no recollection of my feelings about that debate at all, other than that I wanted to make a good argument. (I seem to remember I lost.)

I sometimes wonder whether I became a feminist because of that early experience but it doesn't seem to have taken any of the rest of you that way, so it's obviously not a sufficient explanation. But I do think that while school took my sisters from me it gave me friends as sisters, though I would not have put it that way at the time.

So, dear friend who has come back into my life in our old age, thank you, thank you for that friendship.

With much love, as ever,
Rachel

HEAVY THINGS

Rachel's Journal
31 August
*Went out to see Hannah yesterday and had our usual conversation
about books and grandchildren and politics and gardens. We talked
again about our very different experiences of childhood, hers as a
'red diaper' baby in the Jewish immigrant community of Montreal,
mine in India and that English boarding school. How was it that
we had come to be in the same women's group and that we share so
much?*

*H was asking me again about school and why I have never
talked about it before. She was quite angry with me for not
telling her when we have known each other so long. I've begun
to think about what was unspoken at school, what could never
be said in letters home, and those things which I have refused
to think about, not talked about to anyone – even myself. Chris
tried with Mum and Dad all her life, kept trying to tell them
how she had felt abandoned, but it was hard for them to hear.
Hard for me to hear, too. She and I only found a way to talk
about it at the end.*

She stopped writing and looked around her bedroom for a
moment, as she thought about those long school holidays. It
would be wrong to say that it was all dreadful. If she and Chris and,
later, Jane had been miserable it was in a very humdrum kind of
way. We were not abused or mistreated, she thought. Holidays from
school, especially the times at Auntie May's, were – not awful – but
dreary. And holidays were meant to be so special. She wrote again:

*Chris and I talked about it sitting in the day room at the hospice
not long before she died. She said, 'I think I was depressed for most*

of those years, you know, but it wasn't something I could understand at the time'. And what could our letters home say about what we didn't know ourselves?

Rachel was writing on her knee in bed. The journal was the only writing she did in her own dreadful scrawl. Never mind the young not being able to write properly because of computers. Neither could the old, if she was typical. No one wrote letters now but her journal was a letter, she thought, a letter to herself, in which she tried to reach towards that honesty which all those years of letter writing in the past had made so difficult.

We wanted to make everything okay for Mum and Dad, of course, as children do. We knew they loved us and so we had to protect them from the truth of the hurt they did us. After all, even though I was determined never to send my children away they protected me. I didn't know about the bullying at school until years afterwards. And perhaps, perhaps, our love is always mixed up with other things. We hurt the people we love. Being a parent taught me that. 'Sin' Christians would call it.

When Dad died she had found a couplet from somewhere lodged in her head like one of those tunes they call earworms:

And so through all eternity
I forgive you, you forgive me.

It wasn't even good verse and she had no idea where it came from. She'd look it up sometime.

She turned back to her writing.

Looking back now, I realize that the worst thing about those school years – sometimes moments, sometimes hours when horror descended – was what I called 'my funny breathing'. I could not breathe and could not sit still. I was consumed with the struggle to keep my lungs going, to contain the terror of imminent death. Of course, I never actually talked to anyone about it but it must have been obvious to anyone who was with me when an attack came on. Mum certainly knew about my 'funny breathing'. In fact I think she was the person who named it, as it started that summer just before we were left behind at school and Mum and Dad went back to India with Jane and Jim.

Once in Auntie F's car (her driving was always a cause for some alarm but that wasn't the trigger. I don't know what the trigger was, being in a small space sometimes – or a large space with a lot of people but being unable to get out). Anyway, whatever it was, I was taken with my 'funny breathing' while we were driving along and in the end I cried out to stop the car so I could get out and stand by the side of the road struggling for breath. Mum was there. What happened next? I can't remember. I survived, of course.

What did Mum and Auntie F make of these times? No one ever said anything, though I think Auntie May once told me to pull myself together. But perhaps I misremembered. Once an attack was over and I could breathe again, it became one of those things you didn't talk about.

Emma was telling me the other day about a friend of hers who has panic attacks and as she described them, I suddenly realized that, of course, that is what I had through those years at school. I looked it up on the internet and all my symptoms are there. Now I suppose it would be a case of child psychotherapy or medication but there was no easy handing out of behaviour modifying drugs or talking cures to kids in those days. Was that good or bad? The attacks eased when I was in the Sixth form, perhaps because by then I had those friendships I wrote to Peggy about. I have never had a panic attack since leaving school, so it has sunk down out of memory. So glad. I really don't want to remember.

She stopped writing and flexed the cramp in her fingers. She had said to Peggy that school had given her a lot – and it had. But there was the dark side. Not just the panic attacks but her habit of walking round the school after lights out when it seemed she was the only person in the world who wasn't asleep. Even Peggy didn't know about that. She slept like a log. When did it start? Quite early on in her time there but it went on – she thought – until she was in the Sixth Form and had her friends and was whatever she was then. Older? More secure?

But in those early days at school she would lie awake after lights out unable to sleep way beyond the hours of illegal reading and quiet chatter, until at last a kind of terror would seize her as she lay listening to the soft sounds of breathing, the occasional sleep-talk, from the sleepers. Then sometimes, unable to bear it, she would get up, shuffle on a dressing gown and prowl barefoot through the corridors, passing from the dormitory into old classrooms with their wooden desks, patches of solid darkness in the shadows. She knew which boards creaked and how the biology lab smelled of formaldehyde as she brushed past the benches, braving the dissected dog fish. These solitary explorations were her secret. She did not understand why, but they kept something alive in her, a sense of the shadow side of school which could not be put into words, perhaps.

I was the school ghost, she thought now. She had laid the ghost to rest, blotted it from memory as soon as she left, but on this trip back, as she had walked through the bright airy classrooms which replaced the old dormitories, she had felt a cold air on her back. Just an open window, of course.

She could not possibly have told anyone about it, much less written it in a letter to Mum and Dad. It had been – not forgotten exactly – but certainly not ever allowed to surface. Heavy things underneath, as Mum used to say about packing. But, last time she had seen Jane they had been talking about school and the reunion and she had laughingly told her sister about her midnight prowling. 'Oh I did that, too,' Jane said, and told about how one night when she was about twelve and unable to sleep she had got up and knocked on the door of the deputy housemistress. It was, she thought, very late and she felt that she had been awake for hours but of course her light would have been put out at about 8.00, so it could have been 10.00, not midnight as she had imagined. When Rachel asked what happened, Jane said, 'Oh! She gave me a mug of cocoa and a biscuit and then I went back to bed.' Rachel was impressed. She could no more have knocked on the teacher's door in the night than – well – written to Mum and Dad about it. Now she thought that perhaps she had not been alone, that the dormitories might have been full of ghosts, other girls – dreaming or awake – moving through school in the darkness.

HOLIDAYS

Rachel climbed into the last carriage of the train, somewhat breathless from running down the platform. She tried to push forward through the standing passengers to grab the back of a seat, but the train set off with a jerk, sending her crashing into a young woman. 'Sorry!' The woman briefly opened her eyes, then closed them again to concentrate on the music from her phone. Friday evening rush hour in Liverpool Lime Street. No chance of reading. Rachel thought back over the afternoon. She had been in Liverpool for a workshop, meeting up with a small group of researchers, old colleagues and friends, two of whom had walked with her down to the station. At Lime Street the departures board had shown a train about to leave for Manchester. 'Run,' Henry had said. 'See you soon.' So she had run.

Lime Street Station – scene of so many arrivals and departures when she had been a school girl – was much lighter and brighter than she remembered it. Now on the crowded train she peered out through the bodies, sensing rather than seeing the walls of the cutting through which the train was passing. These dark cliffs, slimy with moisture, filtering any daylight, had always been the signal to settle down for the duration or, coming the other way, to start putting on coats, standing on the seats to get down cases, trying to make sure she had the all the tickets safe in her school purse. Auntie May would regularly retell the story of how she and Chris had once arrived at Lime Street with the return half of one ticket to London between them. Well, Rachel thought now, in defence of that younger self, after all I was only what? Twelve? Thirteen? And it's a long way from Sevenoaks to Liverpool. She and Chris and later Jane as well, would get off the train at Lime Street, stiff from travel, and look for Auntie May. There she would be, umbrella under her arm, wearing her green hat, standing legs slightly akimbo by WHSmiths, ready to take them on the last leg of the journey, the train to Huyton.

They were slowing down at a station. People pushed past to get off. She peered out, but couldn't see a station sign. Damn! In her haste she had jumped onto a stopping train. This would take hours. A couple of stops later she found a seat and peered out. Were they near Huyton? She couldn't see any sign. She sank back and closed her eyes. As she resigned herself to the journey, she remembered how in that other life the long train journeys – London to Newcastle, Newcastle to Liverpool, London to Liverpool and back again – had punctuated the transitions from school to holiday, or rather from school to 'not-school'. They were liminal times which had their own consolations. Rachel and Chris would sit, talking or in silence, but comfortable with each other. Rachel still loved journeys. Travelling, even on the slow train from Liverpool to Manchester was a time out of time. She drifted.

At the end of term excited, almost hysterical, girls would run in and out of cubicles, saying, 'The holiday! The holidays!' 'Goodbye!' 'Will you write to me?' We all knew the script, she thought. We had read the stories. We knew that holidays were meant to be special. And perhaps for some it was genuine excitement but Rachel wondered now whether this was not so much eager anticipation as anxiety about leaving the security of school. At least in school you knew where you were, where you should be at any given moment of day or night; you had timetables, bells, rules, things to do. This suited Rachel aged thirteen; less so aged sixteen, but even then school was secure. 'Holidays' were unpredictable. There were moments of pleasure; a book from the library, a walk in the heather above Granny's house in Northumberland, a game of sevens after tea. But mostly days and nights stretched out in undifferentiated greyness, shot through with anxiety or bewilderment.

At school no one asked, 'Where are you going for your holidays?' We didn't 'go on holiday' she thought but we didn't go home either, if home meant parents, the place you kept the toys of your childhood, the books you knew by heart. 'Holidays' meant guardians, the adults whom their parents had chosen when they returned to Africa or India or wherever they were based. We never spoke of it, Rachel thought, but we knew that guardians were a mixed bag, people who were more or less able to look after us or make sure, at least, that we were fed – no mean thing in the 1950s when rationing lingered and there was not much money.

Her friend Gill's parents had advertised for her guardians in their local church. Somehow Rachel knew that Gill was miserable there, but they never spoke about it. When five years later Gill's parents came home on furlough and left her two younger sisters to join her at school, they must have realised that these were not the best people to care for their children so they sent Gill's sisters to another couple. But they did not send Gill there. She went on her own to the same cold but Christian household.

Rachel thought of the cottage in rural Norfolk where Gill now lived with her husband and a small terrier. They were sitting in their garden when Rachel visited them last and Gill had suddenly said, 'I don't feel I ever got to know my sisters until we were grown up.' Rachel had made a sympathetic noise. 'You know how it was,' Gill said. 'We were not allowed to talk to our sisters in term time, were we? I never understood why. Then I was separated from them in the holidays. At least you were with your sisters in the holidays,' she said to Rachel. 'You were one of the lucky ones.'

Yes, we were the most fortunate of girls, Chris and I, thought Rachel, and we knew it. We had each other and we had Aunties, 'real aunties', both Dad's sisters and Mum's.

She thought of Auntie May, their guardian, Mum's sister, but so much older than Mum. She had been the oldest surviving child and Mum the youngest of that big Irish family. Auntie May had had three boys but they were all dead, two killed in the War and one in that suicide no one spoke of, and here she was now with her sister's children who were all girls. 'I don't know anything about girls,' she would sniff to Mrs Packer, her oldest friend.

Auntie May still called the shops in the centre of Huyton 'the village', but the old rural settlement had long been overtaken, 'overwhelmed' some said, by the high-rise council estates. She had a holly hedge at the front of her tiny garden but she could not keep out the rubbish, the roar of lorries that thundered down the road just feet away, shaking the little red-brick two-up-two-down. The middle of the terrace was the prime position, she always said, because it kept the heat. However, in Rachel's memory the house was always cold except for the few feet around the coal fire in the back room which was kitchen, dining and living room. On the tiled fire-surround was the big coal-scuttle which had to be filled and brought in from the coal shed outside. It loomed huge and heavy in memory but then every chair, every piece of worn lino, every step on the steep flight of stairs to the two bedrooms was as vivid as if she had been there yesterday. She must be near there now? Late summer light showed a flat landscape of stubble fields through the train window.

It was dark that back room, the room they lived in, dark from the huge pear tree that filled the back garden and dark from the brown paint and brown worn furniture with which the room was overfull. Getting across the room to the kitchen was a squeeze what with the table and its three chairs, the sideboard with its dishes, the one armchair by the fire where Auntie May sat after dinner, not to mention the hearth itself. There was one picture, which hung over the table, and that, too, was mainly brown though in a dark gold frame. It was called 'The Toast' and showed a lot of people in old-fashioned clothes standing up with raised glasses around a table covered in food. Rachel and Chris spent hours trying to find the toast among the piles of painted food until Rachel read about 'toasts' and explained to Chris. She wondered now where the picture had come from or why it hung there.

Perhaps Auntie May liked it because it showed a table full of food. She was a good cook, a good manager. She baked all year round, made marmalade in January, bottled fruit in season, laid down eggs to glass in winter when – as everyone knows – the hens don't lay well so eggs get dearer. For some reason Rachel had tried to do that at school once, making up the slimy mixture to coat the eggs which she put into the tin waste bin in her school cubicle. It must have been when they were in the sixth form and had a gas ring in the common room and they had all gone mad on making illegal sweets out of sugar stolen from the dining room and peppermint essence from Boots. The eggs venture didn't work and everyone now assumes you can buy eggs all year round, not to mention strawberries. What would Auntie May have thought?

She was queen of the cooker, which took up most of the space in the tiny kitchen off the back room, a space only big enough for two people if you went side-ways. Just as well she stayed so thin, despite all the baking. On the other side of the side-board from the kitchen was the 'walk-in larder' which was her pride and joy as it had a marble slab, on which rested all the food which needed to be kept cold: the half-eaten joint on Monday, the jug of custard, milk, eggs. One of the worst sins you could commit was to leave the scullery door open so the flies got in.

There were two rooms downstairs but the front room was only for Sundays. Auntie May dusted it on Saturdays. Then, after Church and Sunday lunch while the girls washed up, she shovelled up some burning coals from the back grate and rushed the few feet into the front room shouting, 'Fire! Fire!' and put the coals into the front-room grate, so they could have Sunday tea in there. Rachel wondered now if Auntie May secretly enjoyed going through the house with the flaming coals shouting, 'Fire!'

Mrs Packer always came for Sunday tea. She and Auntie May, who never called each other by their Christian names, would sit in front of the fire with their skirts pulled up, showing their suspenders and stocking tops – 'getting the good of the fire' – while they listened to the Palm Court Orchestra and ate Auntie May's cakes.

The stairs up beside the kitchen were so steep that Rachel and Chris went up on all fours. Their bedroom was at the front and Auntie May's at the back with the bathroom which was over the scullery. It was always cold. Rachel shivered, remembering having their weekly bath. Even in summer it felt cold. In winter she once refused to have one. 'Don't be so nesh,' Auntie May would say. She ran the bath so that you didn't take too much hot water and you could always feel the cold bath on your bottom through the warm water. On Sundays in winter when there was no hot water because of having the fire in the front room Auntie May would sometimes as a treat boil up a kettleful on the gas and pour it into the enamel jug so you could have a warm wash. You had to carry the jug upstairs and pour the water carefully into the basin. 'Always put cold in first, or you'll crack the basin,' she would say. But once Rachel forgot and poured the hot water straight in. A big crack appeared in the bottom of the basin. Auntie May was very cross and ever afterward when Rachel washed her hands she saw the crack she had made in the basin and felt guilty.

Auntie May never smacked them. Like Rachel's parents she was radical in her generation and did not believe in corporal punishment at least not for 'great big girls'. No! They did not smack; they used words instead. 'I am disappointed in you,' Mum would say when we were naughty as children, Rachel remembered. We knew God loved us and we knew our parents loved us and we did not want to disappoint them. Guilt, disappointment. She looked at the crack in the basin every day of the holidays as she washed her hands and face. What? Will these hands ne'er be clean?

When they had been small children in India there was a ritual of punishment and repentance after wrong-doing. Mum would say, 'I am disappointed in you,' and then you promised not to be naughty again. More serious misdemeanours were dealt with differently. You would be sent to stand in the spare-room bathroom until you were ready to come out. Then Mum would ask, 'What do you say?' to which the right answer was, 'I am sorry.' 'What does sorry mean?' Mum would ask, to which the answer was, 'It means I won't do it again.'

The spare-room bathroom was a dark concrete box, dimly lit by filtered sunlight. Of course, there was no fixed bath or WC as there was no running water. There must have been a basin on a wooden stand, a tin tub propped against a wall, and a couple of what were called 'potties' but which Rachel realised now were commodes, though the word had only entered her vocabulary years later in connection with old age and illness. She knew these must be in the bathroom but all she could remember was the smell of damp and the feel of the low concrete ridge which ran round one corner of the floor in so that when you emptied the bath tub the water did not flood the room but ran out through the drain pipe. Though the semi-darkness and dank air were unpleasant what made the bathroom terrifying was that a snake might climb up the drainpipe while she stood there not wanting to move in case she trod on something or fell over the ridge on the floor. Hers was not a completely unfounded fear. Snakes did sometimes come into the house through the drainpipes and Rachel knew all about cobras.

Though she could not remember any specific naughtiness which was punished in this way, the memory of the room was so sharp that Rachel knew she must have found herself there more than once, even though her main aim from early in life was to be a good girl, not to be a disappointment to her parents. Her younger sister, Jane, was braver. Once she had been shut in the bathroom and when she announced herself ready to come out, Mum said the usual words, 'Jane, I am disappointed in you. What do you say?' Instead of the proper formula Jane had wrinkled her forehead and said, 'Mummy, I am very disappointed in *you*' - at which Mum had burst out laughing.

'Manchester Oxford Road, next station stop.' The tannoy announcement brought Rachel back to the present. Perhaps she should get out the old cabin trunk from under the spare-room bed and have a root around among the old letters. There might be some which had survived among those she wrote on that table in Auntie May's back room under 'The Toast'. She had also, she remembered now, started writing at least one novel. Reading and writing, there was not always a lot to do at Auntie May's. But she always put food on the table, Rachel thought, and that was probably quite a struggle.

> *Huyton*
> *August 15th 1952*
> *Dear Daddy and Mummy,*
> *Thank you for your letters. It is holidays now and we had a nice time at Granny's. Now we are at Auntie May's, so there is not much to write about. I have got a library ticket for the Adult section. I am reading Georgette Heyer. Did you know that your birthday is the same as Mary Queen of Scots, Daddy? I wish mine was. We are waiting for Auntie May's friend Mrs Packer to come round for Sunday tea. She is very nice. She laughs a lot and says she is a scouse, not Irish like Auntie May. Chrissie was not very well this week but Auntie May said there was nothing wrong with her and she was not to stay in bed. Chris says she sends her love and she will write to you next Sunday.*
> *Love,*
> *Rachel*

Rachel was sitting on the spare room floor looking through the bundle of old airmail forms she had picked out of the pile in the trunk. Under them was a cheap notebook which she flipped open. Lined pages filled with her round schoolgirl hand.

HOLIDAYS

Rachel's Journal
PRIVATE. KEEP OUT.
3 April 1954
We are in Huyton again at Auntie May's. There is nothing to do here. We had fish because it is Friday. I wish we could have stayed longer in Northumberland. At least there we can go out for a walk. We had quite a nice time there last summer. Wish Daddy was coming back this summer.

10 April
I have decided that I am going to write a novel, so I am going to the village to buy another notebook. I don't like going to the Post Office now ever since Mr Green squeezed my breasts and slobbered over me that time when we were on a coach trip with the church. I am trying to avoid him, even though I know he can't do anything in the shop with Mrs Green there and people going in and out. I said to Auntie May that I didn't like Mr Green and she said, 'Why ever not? He's such a gentleman.' I'll go down to Woolworths. I wish we knew someone our age here. Glad we are going back to school soon.

14 April
Chrissie is having one of her moods today when she won't talk or do anything. Auntie May has gone out to a Mothers' Union meeting at the Church. She is always going to meetings and talking about India, though she was only there for about two months that time she came out with us after James was born. She is the great India expert now. She always tells how the Indians burn cow dung. That seems to shock the old Mothers' Union people. What boring lives they lead. Boring!

18 April
Easter Sunday and Mummy's birthday. I hope the letter I wrote got there. We went to church and dinner was roast lamb and roast potatoes and apple pie and evaporated milk ('cream so called', as Auntie May says every Sunday). When Chris and I had washed up, Mrs P. came and we had the fire in the front room. Chrissie and I wheeled in the trolley with all Auntie May's cakes on (Coconut pyramids are my favourite) and we listened to the Palm Court Orchestra.

There are some of Auntie May's husband's books in the front room. I found a Complete Works of Shelley there last week, a red leather copy with that very thin paper they use for Bibles. Auntie said I could read it as long as I washed my hands and didn't take it out of the front room. Under the book shelf is the little table where she keeps the photos of our cousins, Harold and Robbie, with their medals and the Gurkha knife that Harold had in the war and the picture of Auntie May and Mrs Packer going to Buckingham Palace to get the medal from the Queen that Robbie won for gallantry. I like the front room in the summer when it is sunny. Sometimes when Auntie May is out I creep in, being careful not to rearrange anything and look at the photos and the backs of the books in the book case.

20 April 1954
We are going back to school tomorrow. I'll be quite pleased in a way. I'll see my friends and it's better than here anyway. I have had a huge row with Auntie May because I told her I needed a bra and she won't let me have one. She says no one wore bras in her day. No surprise. They didn't need them in the ark. I didn't say that of course. Just said I was the only girl in my class still wearing a vest and a liberty bodice and it was embarrassing. Then she started going on about proper corsets but I told her no one at school wore corsets like hers. I am NOT going to wear a corset. I said I would write to Mum and Dad but of course they won't write back for ages and I'll go back to school again without a bra. I can't keep pretending to have my period every week when games lesson comes up. Miss Power says she has her eye on me.

Chrissie and I went for a cycle ride yesterday. We went further than we have ever been before right out into the country to where there is a huge coal tip and a mine. We had quite a nice day just going along and not talking much. I won't see her again properly until the summer now because of school.

Did she ever write that novel? Rachel picked up the notebook with the Journal and put the letters back into the trunk.

Once when she and Chris had been sitting in the day room of the hospice, Chris had started to talk about those holidays at Auntie

May's, about the feeling of claustrophobia induced by the cluttered back room and about those conventions which dictated that the sunniest, most pleasant room in the house could only be used on Sunday afternoons.

'Wasn't it sad?' she said. 'But then, she'd had a sad life, hadn't she, Auntie May? And I was depressed most of the time I think.' Just then a nurse came in and asked if they wanted a cup of tea and a piece of cake. 'Not as good as Auntie May's,' they agreed, but Rachel ate all hers.

'But Granny's was mostly okay, wasn't it?' Rachel had said. For Auntie May was not their only auntie nor were all their holidays in Huyton. For a few days each Christmas and each summer holiday, Rachel and Chris, and in later years Jane, would cross London, not to Euston for the Liverpool train, but to King's Cross for the east coast line to Newcastle to go to Dad's family, their Granny and their other aunties. Auntie Faith would meet them at the station with her car and drive them the thirty miles to Rothbury. She was their only relative with a car. When at last you drove through the village, past the church, the green and the shops, and then began to climb up the County Bank, you knew you were nearly there – the grey stone house with white windows where Granny lived. And there she would be in her dark long skirt, asking if you were all right.

The house was warm and bright. The garden stretched up the hill behind. From the front windows you could look across the valley to the 'Frogs' Eyes', whose proper name was the Simonside Hills, and look down, down to the river Coquet which curved through the valley. It was quiet. The only sound was wood pigeons cooing in their Geordie accents, or so Dad said. Twice during the five years he had come back for two or here days on his way to Geneva or America and then Rachel and Chris were so happy, walking with him through the garden and out onto the moor, talking and talking.

'It was great when Dad came,' she had said to Chris in that hospice room. 'But he always went again, didn't he, after a couple of days?' He left and somehow it was worse than if he had not come and they knew it would be years until he came again. But in that moment it was – well – Dad loved Rothbury and Rachel loved it too, especially the garden which had been made by the Grandad they had never seen. He had bought the house in the 1920s and with it an acre of rough hillside covered in bracken and rocks where he made a garden. Now it was overgrown and untended but they loved it the more for that. There was a high fence at the top to keep out the sheep but if you opened the gate you could walk for miles across the moors on Lord Armstrong's road, a tarmac track which didn't really go anywhere but which Daddy once told Rachel had been built by the unemployed ship-workers in the 1930s, before she was born, when Grandpa lost all his money. But, after all, Rachel thought, he still had the house and garden.

Rothbury in the summer meant picnics. Both their aunties would be there, Auntie Faith and Auntie Nan. The aunties both enjoyed picnics, though they argued about everything else: whether it would rain today, whether modern literature was utterly corrupt, whether they should have fish paste or meat paste sandwiches. Rachel and Chris did not join the arguments. They wore their n-- brown school gabardines whatever the weather, helped to make the sandwiches, which in Rachel's memory were more often fish than meat paste, and went where the aunts had eventually agreed they should go, which more often than not was the Simonsides. Granny never came on picnics. Seated by the fire in her dark long skirts, she never left the house except to be driven to church on Sunday but she was younger than I am now, thought Rachel.

Those picnics! They would go in Auntie F's car and then walk up past the Ancient British camp, up past the preacher's rock where people used to give sermons (more fun than church, Rachel thought to herself).If it was raining they would huddle as far under the rock as they could while they ate their sandwiches but if it was fine they might scramble up right to the high ridge of the Simonside itself and sit there in the heather, smelling the honey scent, munching sandwiches and looking down at the valley, green and far below.

Auntie N would sit in the heather and smoke, telling Rachel and Chris about the ancient Britons and cup-and-ring marked rocks and excavations. She had wanted to be an archaeologist but girls couldn't be archaeologists, so she was a social worker. Auntie F was a teacher. Rachel thought she might be a teacher before she got married. Chris wanted to get married and have lots of children – fourteen, she said. But that was when they were first left at home to go to the aunties for holidays. Later she said she wanted to be a nurse.

Rachel could not disentangle the memories: the walks, the picnics, the times reading books from Granny's book case or from the Huyton library, the boredom, Auntie May's dark kitchen. When Rachel was in the Sixth Form Mum brought Jane home to go to school. 'You'll have to look after Jane, now, as well as keeping an eye on Christine,' Mummy said to Rachel. She and Dad didn't stay but went back to India with James. So now there were three of them for holidays. Auntie May said Rachel should move into the attic space which was up a sort of ladder stairs and was boarded over. There was a low bed right under the sloping roof of the house with a swinging light bulb. Rachel missed Chris being there at night and the talks they used to have but she had a space of her own and, anyway, Chris was different now. But, then, so was she. Everything was the same but different.

They talked about it in those last few weeks when Chris was dying. So many people wanted to see her but sometimes Rachel was the only one there. She would sit by the bed or read quietly out loud to Chris, who lay asleep, or at least with her eyes closed, more and more as time went on and the morphine dose was increased. But those first couple of weeks she had more energy and they would talk and talk.

'Do you remember those Sunday evenings at school when we all had to sit in absolute silence, almost without breathing, while Miss B read to us?'

'Do you remember that holiday when we were sent to the farm?'

'It was awful, wasn't it? But it sounded, well, like something out of Enid Blyton … Our Famous Farm Holiday!'

'Did Mum and Dad ever know about it?'

'Not till later and then only a sanitised version, of course.'

'What was that all about, anyway? We were going to Granny's as usual. Auntie F met us off the train then on the way she suddenly left the usual road and started saying we couldn't go to Granny's. She wouldn't explain, except to say that she had to go to an MRA conference and couldn't look after us. I was really worried about Granny, that she was very ill or something. What year was that?'

'1955? 56?' Rachel said. 'Jane was there so …'

'… the three of us were dropped off in this cottage with the young couple who were hardly there. Then she – Auntie F – just drove off. Not a word! It was awful, wasn't it?' said Chris. 'We had no idea where we were, no money, no map. No phones then of course. We were just dumped, weren't we, like luggage.'

'Well,' said Rachel, 'the young couple who lived there were obviously just married and needed money and she did try to feed us, didn't she?'

'Left a note on the table saying, "your tea is in the sink". Do you remember?'

Rachel remembered it clearly, being confronted with three large fish which needed gutting and scaling and cooking on a peat range. Throughout that week she had felt she ought to be able to manage the situation, make it good for her sisters. After all, she was fifteen, going on sixteen, a competent young woman. She could plot a walk across moorland with a one inch Ordinance Survey map, navigate the London Underground or the national railway system, and discuss *A Portrait of the Artist as a Young Man* but suddenly she was infantilised, powerless. She did not know where they were or why they were there. Did anyone know where they were? Auntie F did, but she was in Switzerland at an MRA conference. Granny? Her behaviour had been becoming increasingly erratic with what Rachel realised now must have been the onset of the dementia of her end years. The previous summer Rachel had been woken a couple of times in the night and gone out to find Granny, her long grey hair unravelled, standing by the airing cupboard on the landing muttering to herself as she counted the sheets and towels. Auntie F had appeared, told Rachel sharply to go back to bed, and taken Granny back to her room. Did Mum and Dad know where they were? Rachel was sure they did not, but a letter to them would take days and anyway what could they do?

Rachel had felt, on those bright August days, as she had when she had stood in the dark bathroom in India. She wanted to come out and say, 'I am sorry. I won't do it again.' Whatever 'it' was.

Rachel had never gutted a fish. The three fish had turned glassy eyes on her from the sink. Jane burst into tears and Chris said, 'I am going to bed. I don't want any tea.'

'I do remember those fish!' she said to Chris. 'How could I forget them?' They could laugh now, even in that hospice room.

'They tasted quite good in the end, I seem to remember,' Chris said. 'Mind you, we were hungry.'

'Just as well! I made a right mess of them but I had never done it before.'

'Course you hadn't. You were great! But what was all that about, not letting us go to Granny's, not telling us anything, not telling Mum and Dad? Dumping us miles from anywhere with no map and no money?'

'I did try to talk to Dad about it and he told me they assumed we were at Granny's, never knew anything about it until we wrote. My sense ...'

'Well?' Chris sank further into the bed.

'Well, you know, did Auntie F really like us? Why should she? Poor her! She was the youngest so was left looking after the mother she had never got on with. There was her brother off being a famous missionary. Then his kids, us, were landed on her. Of course, she was deeply into MRA.'

'Yes, of course! Moral Re-Armament!'

'Yes, and MRA demanded all sorts of absolutes in its followers: purity, absolute honesty, absolute love. So, she had to love us but why should she?! I think that holiday it all got too much for her. Our arrival was going to stop her going to her MRA Conference which, I am sure, she convinced herself was a greater good. Poor her!'

'Hmmm!' said Chris. 'Poor us, too.'

'Yes, but do you remember when we got back to Huyton after that dreadful week, Auntie May had cooked us her Irish version of the all-in-one-pot bacon and cabbage and potatoes dinner and seemed really pleased to see us.'

A 'GOOD EDUCATION'?

Rachel was walking along by the river. Her southern friends and family never quite believed her when she said she could walk out of her house into the Mersey Valley Country Park and go for miles without crossing a road. Not a dark satanic mill in sight. The swallows dipped and swung over the water, flying low, which meant low pressure. Summer would soon be over. The rose bay willow herb was showing purple along the edge of the Ees and the berries on the rowan above the path were beginning to redden.

'Oh the oak and the ash and the bonny rowan tree,' Rachel hummed to herself, hearing her father's voice in her head. 'They-ey flourish at home in my own country.' This was her own country, now, as she always felt when she visited the south.

The school reunion and her continuing email correspondence with Peggy had stirred up in Rachel memories whose clarity and detail astonished her. She could almost smell the ghosts of long-boiled cabbage which had pervaded the school corridors. Though she'd never noticed it at the time, there must have been other odours, given the infrequent bath times which were the rule. At Kodai there had been communal showers on Saturdays but nobody had showers in England. ('It's an American habit,' somebody had told her. The unspoken disapproval hovered in the air.) How those classrooms must have stunk, with all those young bodies only bathing and changing their clothes once a week!

Oh! And those dreadful buckets of bloody cloths in which you had to fish around for your knickers if a period had come on you unexpectedly, as Rachel's so often did. Rachel had her first period just before she started at WH. Mum had shown her how to put on the bulky towel, held in place with safety pins and Dad had said, 'If you were an Indian girl we would be having a celebration now because you would be regarded as a woman.' But no one else spoke of these things. She had only found out about the buckets by asking Gill with whom she shared a cubicle. Half her pocket money, she seemed to remember, went on buying STs and most of the rest on church collections.

She crossed the brook which fed into the Mersey at this point. The balsam was flowering, pink and exotic, almost choking the brook's narrow passage. Two runners came past. She sometimes felt an oddity on this path, since she was neither a runner nor a dog-owner. She usually kept a good pace but today she was abstracted, afflicted by memories.

That day – was it their second day at school? – when she and Chris had been called early out of the afternoon lesson to say good bye. Every detail of the scene was clear in Rachel's memory except her own feelings. She and Chris had stood together by the brick arch, which marked the boundary between school and the rest of the world, and watched as Mum and Dad walked away along the suburban street, turning now and then to wave. Was Mum crying? Rachel thought so, and Jane was running beside her, trying to keep up on her short legs and tugging at her hand. Dad held James's hand. They turned at the corner and waved, 'Goodbye. Goodbye.' Then they were gone. Chris and Rachel had to go back into school. It was time for tea. Chris was crying, big sobs. Rachel took her sister's hand. Was she sad, too? She supposed, looking back, that she must have been. Did she comfort Chris? She hoped so, but she couldn't remember. She feared she had not. How often she had failed in the task which had been hers since she could remember, to 'look after your little sister'?

They had walked back through the big front door which was really only for visitors but they didn't know that then. They didn't know that you had to use the side door to go in and out of the building. It was one of those rules that they would internalize before the term was out.

There was a tall girl standing in the hall near the door into the Dining Room. 'What are you girls doing?' she said crossly. 'You're late for tea. Go on in. Then she looked again. 'You're new aren't you? Do you know your tables?'

'Yes,' Rachel said.

She wished she and Chris could sit together but sisters weren't allowed to be at the same table. She leaned against the big heavy doors with their brass handles and they went into the dining hall. The noise of everyone talking was like a wave. You had to push into it. There were big long tables with about twelve girls sitting at each. The older girls were at the top, the youngest at the bottom near the big metal teapot.

They found their places and Rachel sat down quietly hoping no one would notice her. There was something on her plate but she didn't feel hungry. She nibbled a bit and drank some tea and then it was time to pass the plates down to the bottom of the table, so that they could be cleared up.

'Don't you want it?' The girl next to Rachel asked, nodding at the plate. She had been talking to someone on the other side of her. She had red hair and freckles. Rachel didn't know her name.

'Not really.'

'Can I have it?' Rachel pushed the plate towards her and she forked it in rapidly. Everyone was getting up and pushing in their chairs.

'Where do we go now?' Rachel asked the girl. She knew you had to be somewhere because every minute of the day you had to be somewhere. The girl looked surprised.

'Study time now,' she said. 'You're in my class, aren't you? We're in Room 4.' Room 4, where was that? Rachel couldn't remember. She felt a tremor of panic. 'I'll show you,' the girl said, not unkindly.

They went into the study room where girls were banging desks and talking loudly, taking books out of lockers and looking confidently about them. Rachel found a desk and tried to remember what she was meant to be doing. Where were her books? She had put them into a locker somewhere. She began opening lockers at random, trying to find her books.

'Settle down now, girls,' said the teacher coming in and sitting down at her desk, which was on a sort of platform at the front. Rachel found her books and sat at a desk towards the back as the hubbub died down.

A prefect put her head round the door. 'Rachel Newby?'

'Rachel Newby?' the teacher asked, 'Is Rachel here?' Rachel gulped and put up her hand. What had she done?

'Piano practice', said the prefect. 'You're down for this slot. Didn't you know?' Rachel followed her out of the room.

'Do you know where to go?'

'No, please.'

'I'll show you, but remember tomorrow.' And she led the way back past the dining hall to a row of doors from behind which came the sounds of scales and someone stumbling over a line of notes. She opened a door into a room just big enough for a piano and a stool. 'Here you are,' she said. 'Where's your music?'

'I haven't had a lesson yet.'

'Oh well, just do some scales or something and then go back to the study room.'

That was at the beginning. The not knowing where you were, the sense of being out of place. She felt them again as present terrors. But later she had found the routine came easily. It held her. She liked the regularity, she liked the lessons, all except maths where she sat at the back and giggled with Peggy when Miss Clarke said yet again, 'Now watch the board and I'll go frew it.'

One year they had a new maths teacher and slowly Rachel began to understand something about the pattern and regularity of number. Light broke through here and there and she thought, 'I could do this.' But that teacher left at the end of the year and the fog descended again.

Then there was games, of course and – in that first year - needlework.

'Haven't you ever seen a sewing machine before?' The teacher was stern and her eyes sharp. Rachel thought of squatting on the cool concrete with Chris and watching as the tailor, cross-legged on the veranda floor, fed the cloth smoothly under the darting needle, his other hand turning the wheel of his machine. And the bazaar with the men sitting in the front of the shop, the bright colours of the material under their brown hands. She gulped.

'Yes, Miss, but I've never threaded one.'

'Well, it's time you learned. Show her, please, someone.' But Rachel's 'fingers were all thumbs', as Auntie May would have said. She never was much good at needlework, whether machining or hand-stitching, though later in life she had managed to do simple tasks like making curtains. And she had always been a good darner, the one domestic skill she had learned in Kodai.

Of course, Rachel thought, I spent most of that first year being ill and lying in sick bay reading and then, because I was in the top half of the class in end of year exams, I went into the Latin set and didn't have to do needlework or domestic science – that was for the dimmies.

She turned away from the river to walk over the football fields back to the house. Did I have a 'good education'? she wondered. That's what Mum and Dad wanted for us, why they sent us 'home'. An all-girls' school where your women teachers expected you to work, where there were no distractions (which she supposed meant boys), homework time strictly managed and overseen, being a teenager not yet invented. Bookish girl that she was, it had suited her.

Some of the teaching was – well – Latin for example! (Lat'n, as Auntie May always called it.) Rachel thought of Miss Jones who even at A level dictated to them her own florid translations of the set texts which you learned by heart and hoped that somehow you would recognize enough of the exam piece to be able to rattle it off. You had to pass Lat'n to get into 'a good university' to read an arts subject. We loved Miss Jones because she told a good story – sometimes even about other teachers but all those years of doing Latin even into her first year of undergraduate study and yet I couldn't translate a line of Livy now if you paid me, she thought. At least all the hours of practising in the monk-like music cells had meant she could still sit down and play the piano, more or less. She was having lessons again, playing Mozart trios with two friends. They called themselves 'The Geriatrics'.

But, she thought, crossing the road and going through the gate into her local park, we did have wonderful teachers in History and English. Learning by heart was not only Latin and French irregular verbs but chunks of poetry, a resource that lasted now into old age and kept opening out into new delights. And – here she struck across the grass – I got to University, had a room of my own, could get into the Library. She caught a glimpse of a woman in a long coat moving away from her through the formal gardens. The ghost of Virginia Woolf, perhaps. Rachel smiled to herself.

Of course, school assumed that all its pupils would get married. Education was to make you a better wife and mother. If somehow you failed at this basic female task, then you became a teacher. The 'top set' didn't do domestic science but it was assumed that somehow you would learn how to cook and do the domestic labour. Or perhaps it was really about class as well as gender. Education was still modelled on the pre-war assumption that middle-class women would have domestic servants. After all, Rachel thought, Mum had been a graduate, but when she got married – no, when she got engaged – she had to stop. When our first child was born, I had to stop working as a teacher. But it was the early 1970s. I went back to work, wanted to use my intellectual training, joined the women's movement. So school gave us the tools but discouraged us from using them. Hard to believe now what a man's world it was. That time I went in to hire a telly - was it 1968? – and they told me I had to get my husband to sign for it. Peter was doing his post-graduate study and I was the one bringing in the money but a wife couldn't sign a financial document, not even a TV rental. She stumbled a little, remembering how she had kicked up a fuss in the shop and stomped out without the telly.

What would have happened if we had stayed in Kodai? She had never dared think about it through all those years. It wasn't only about race since, after all, when we were at school in Kodai all the pupils were white; Americans, Norwegians, Dutch, a few Brits, like us. She realized now that Mum and Dad were following the old practice of the Raj, believing that the model of the English boarding school must be the best for their children, even though – as she had discovered only from reading his autobiography – Dad had been miserable when he was sent to boarding school. And he went home for the holiday.

In her street now she waved to a neighbour across the road. Audre Lorde argued that the master's tools cannot be used to dismantle the master's house. But perhaps if you know what tools there are, you can look for others. Or is that the argument of privilege? I was taught to read 'like a man', she thought, but at least I knew how to read, so in the company of other women, whether flesh and blood or paper and ink, I could learn to read – how? – against the grain? Differently? 'As a woman'? Yes; but it took time for her to re-discover what her 'good education' blinded her to for a while, that she read as a white woman, a post-colonial, white woman; something she had understood in some profound way, ever since she had lain under the mosquito net on the veranda of the bungalow and heard below the sweep-sweep of the untouchable woman's broom. And now, she thought, opening her gate, I am an old woman.

Her tiny front garden was full of old-fashioned cottage plants. Lady's mantle and lavender sprawled across the path to her front door. She picked a lavender spike and breathed in the scent as she turned the key. She was home.

VII

ENDINGS AND BEGINNINGS
(December 1956–1957)

'A COLD COMING
WE HAD OF IT'

'Letter for you.' The letter-monitor dropped the white envelope by Rachel's plate and went on down the table handing out yesterday's post. This was not the usual blue Indian airmail form or even one of the airmail envelopes with the stripy edges and real letters inside on special airmail paper which Dad favoured. Mum's writing was easy to read. Dad always typed. He said no one could read his scrawl, but it also meant that he could do a general letter to everyone, including Granny and the aunts, all on carbon copies, to which he added a little message specially to you on the bottom of your copy. An Indian letter had come just yesterday with its month-old news.

No. The crisp white envelope on her plate today had an Oxford postmark. Rachel picked it up, her fingers trembling. You were not allowed to open letters at breakfast. You had to take them upstairs to read in the few minutes between the end of breakfast and the start of lessons. 'Meal times are for conversation,' Miss Burroughs said.

At the signal, 'You may go', Rachel followed the press of girls into the corridor, secretly easing open the seal. An hour later she was in the Head's office.

'Do you have a suit?'

'No, Miss Burroughs.' Miss Burroughs must have known she didn't have a suit. You were allowed two outfits other than your school uniform, a skirt and pullover which you changed into after school on weekdays and wore on Saturdays, and a best dress for Sundays. 'No, Miss Burroughs', she said, again, 'I have a Sunday dress, but no suit.'

'You can't go for an interview at Oxford without a suit. Go and have a word with Matron.'

'Yes, Miss Burroughs.'

'What about a hat? You must have a hat.'

'I do, Miss Burroughs. Auntie May bought me one in the summer.' She thought of the vomit-green hat with its little veil and feather, which Auntie May had insisted she buy. Rachel had stuffed it into a brown paper bag and crushed it into the back of the school locker which still functioned as her wardrobe, book store and writing desk as well as the stand for the basin.

'Gloves? You must have gloves.'

'Yes, Miss Burroughs.' She had no intention of wearing gloves, so did not mention that she only had one.

'Very well. Matron will find you a suit.'

So it was that she set off for Oxford in a pink suit with box pleats. It was several sizes too large, but she kept it up with a narrow brown belt, also provided by Matron. Rachel wondered where the pink suit had come from. She carried a small case and a brown paper bag in which the green hat nestled. She could not refuse the suit but at least she could make sure she never wore the hat.

The train rattled through the Kentish countryside. Winter trees stretched, twiggy against a grey sky. She still found the landscape of England shocking, though she had made this journey to and from boarding school so many times. She could recite the litany of station names: Elmstead Woods, Grove Park, Hither Green … Mysterious places where people led unimaginable lives, fathers who got on the train each morning and came back each evening. She thought of the bungalow in India, the slashes of unbearable light coming through the gaps in the tatties around the veranda, the glare of sun beyond. She shivered suddenly but whether from cold or from a sudden stab of home-sickness for that world she could not tell. There was only one other person in the carriage, a middle-aged woman sitting in the opposite corner, reading a book. Rachel's small case was slung on the nets overhead just above a faded oval picture of Windsor Castle.

Oxford station did not look like the entrance to the promised land. It was a grey December afternoon and raining heavily. As she looked for the right bus stop in the station fore-court, the paper on which she had written the bus numbers got more and more sodden. So did the paper bag with the hat in it, which was crushed against the suitcase in her other hand. She longed to throw the hat into a rubbish bin.

At last she found the bus and it trundled up towards north Oxford. She rubbed the steamed up windows and peered out into the gloom but couldn't make out much beyond damp pavements and ordinary looking streets. The bus lurched into a wide open space and passed more buildings and a church. Then the conductor shouted out her stop. She was given a room of her own, a student bedroom with a narrow bed and a desk. She imagined herself unpacking books and putting them onto the shelves. There was a meal in hall which she ate in a daze. All the girls around her seemed to be with someone they knew. They all seemed so confident.

'Where are you from?' the girl next to her, who had been talking in a high voice to her neighbour, turned to Rachel suddenly.

'Um. Walthamstow Hall,' said Rachel blushing.

'Oh. I haven't heard of that school. I'm at Roedean. Do we play you at hockey?'

'I don't know. I don't think so.' She tried to remember the names of schools she had heard Chris talk about. Chris would have known. She was the games player.

The girl gave her a hard look and turned back to her neighbour.

Next morning there were interviews. The other girls were all obviously wearing their own suits. They wore expertly applied lipstick and court shoes. As Rachel waited outside the Principal's Office for the first interview the girl sitting next to her turned to her. 'I always buy my shoes in Ital-ay,' she drawled. 'It's the only place for shoes, don't you think?' At that moment Rachel was called for interview. Her school lace-ups squeaked on the parquet floor.

She never remembered how she had got back to school. For the next two weeks she lay awake at night rehearsing the brilliant answers she had failed to give. One interview had not gone well but she thought she had done okay on T. S. Eliot. 'Midnight shakes the memory.' She watched the moonlight streaming through the uncurtained windows onto the walls of the cubicle. The noise of other sleepers in the dormitory, little sighs and the occasional snore, comforted her. She did not, as she had in the past, get up and walk around the school in the dark. She felt she was too old for that now, too responsible. She was about to leave school. It was her last term, nearly her last week. She had stayed on a term after all her friends so that she could do the Oxford entrance. Margaret was at Manchester now, sending Rachel letters full of news of student parties and finding her way round a strange city. Peggy's mother had said she wanted Peggy at home for a few months and she wrote too, grumbling about her mother and writing wickedly funny accounts of working in Sharp's Toffee Factory where she had found a job so that she could go abroad in the summer. She and Rachel had plans to have an adventure together but now Rachel was left behind, stranded, an earlier life form like those creatures Micky had taught them about in O level Biology who didn't adapt and so died out. She wished she had left with the others. This last term she had been an anomaly, missing her friends and working on her own, writing essays for Mrs Hill and then sitting exams upstairs all by herself in a cold room at the top of the school.

And she didn't want to think about what was going to happen when she left. She had to get a job but what could she do and, more important, she had to get somewhere to live. She couldn't go to Granny's obviously and Auntie May had told Mum and Dad she couldn't go there. She had been looking for a live-in job but how do you look for that? No one at school knew. The two other girls who were trying for Oxford and Cambridge were day girls who lived at home with their parents.

It was Auntie N who had suggested Rachel find a job in a children's home, so she had written to the London County Council and was waiting to hear from them. It might be okay to be in London and she liked children. She shifted in the bed, feeling the springs sticking into her, thinking sleep would never come, but when the ten to seven bell rang she found she had, after all, fallen asleep and she just wanted to turn over and sleep some more, not get up and go down to the chatter and clatter of breakfast in the dining hall.

It was two days before the end of the Christmas term and there was still no word from Oxford. Only two more breakfasts. In the dining room with its long tables and portraits of past head-mistresses, the noise rose. A girl at another table began to laugh hysterically. Rachel was not listening. She must hear from Oxford before the Christmas holiday. She looked around for her sisters. She couldn't see Jane's blonde head but there was Chris at the next table, her mouth half-open and a far-away look in her eyes. Rachel felt the usual mixture of irritation and protective love. She had not really spoken to Chrissie all term. She had found her on the stairs yesterday in the few moments between afternoon lessons and evening prep and given her the latest letter from India.

'You okay?'

'Hmm.'

'Nearly Christmas.'

'Yes.'

Mum and Dad wrote of how glad they were she was getting 'a good education', and she wrote back, sitting on her bed in the dormitory, about the lessons she was doing and how the exams had gone. She did not say anything about feeling left behind, the only one still at school. She did not talk to them about what she would do after she left.

'Letter for you.'

Rachel took the envelope and felt a surge of such strong feeling that she put it down hastily and drank some tea. She was a prefect. She could not get up and run upstairs to open the letter, but must continue sitting at the top of the table.

'What is it?' The girl next to her asked.

'Oh! Nothing. More tea, please.'

She passed her cup down the long table. The girls on 'her' table this term were a real mixed bag. When she had looked on the board at the start of term and seen who she'd been assigned she had groaned inwardly, turning to say something to Peggy before she remembered that of course Peggy wasn't there but was getting up to go to her shift in the factory and Margaret was in Manchester being a student and sitting where she liked. Still, it was nearly her last meal. The youngest girl, the one at the bottom of the table near the tea pot was called Jennifer, a skinny child with a perpetual cold. She probably had one now as her nose and eyes were red. She stood up to lift the heavy metal tea pot. Some prefects would have told her to 'sit down' but Rachel remembered too well being that confused little girl who was suddenly expected to saw neat slices off the loaf or pour the tea without slopping. She saw that the girl's tie was coming undone and thought of her own struggles with the unfamiliar uniform. All those clothes to wear and still to be perpetually cold. 'Thank you,' she said down the table and smiled at the girl.

At that moment the loudspeakers in each corner clicked on and the eight o'clock news on the BBC home service began, the regular morning routine. No more talking now, only the clatter of cutlery. Miss Burroughs said it was good for her 'gels' to hear the news each morning and in these last few months Rachel had listened avidly. It felt as if the whole world outside the confines of School was shifting. How they had argued, she and the others in the common room, about the invasion of Suez and the merits of Anthony Eden. How could Britain, how could 'we', behave like this? The 'Suez Crisis' they were calling it, but the rage Rachel felt at the news from Egypt astonished her. Where had it come from, this hot anger? She remembered the Suez Canal from that last voyage back from India, the orange desert stretching to the sharp line of the horizon. She had been out on deck and had seen – or perhaps thought she had seen – in the distance a line of camels with men in flowing robes. Was this rage something to do with India and all the debates at home about Independence?

Then had come the stirrings of revolt in Hungary. She and Peggy, not content with the compulsory dose of news at breakfast, had tuned in every evening on the crackling wireless in the sixth-form common room to hear the latest on the uprising. Students only a year or two older than she was had confronted the Soviet might, demanded freedom, asked the world to intervene. But the world had turned its back. The Soviet tanks had rolled. Winter set in.

But this morning Rachel didn't care if nuclear war broke out. Oxford shimmered before her. 'Please, God! Let me have got in.'

Eventually, 8.10, the end of the news. 'Plates should be passed to the bottom of the table in silence.' When the clatter had died down, Miss Thomson, the member of staff on duty, gave the signal, 'You may go'.

At last she could go up to the dormitory. As a prefect she had a cubicle of her own. The wooden walls were just six feet high and Peggy grumbled that it was all right for midgets like Rachel but what about normal human beings who could more or less see over the top. At least it had a door you could close.

She tore at the envelope and read the paper frantically, trying to make sense of it. '… very able candidates this year … competition … sorry to tell you …' Somehow she had known it. Sobs rose up in her. She stifled them as best she could, falling onto the bed, her face in the pillow. Gradually through her tears she heard a scrabbling sound, a giggle. Those fourth formers in the next cubicle again. It was nearly time for lessons to begin. She sat up and looked for the skimpy towel which hung on the wash-stand jammed into the corner between the bed and the door. There was still some cold water in the washstand bowl. She could hear the girl who was water-monitor this week working her way up the dormitory, emptying the basins. She'd be here in a moment. Rachel splashed her face. The scrabbling sound returned and two faces appeared over the top of the cubicle. 'Get down,' she said and they slid down, giggling. Rachel fled down the corridor to the toilets, rattled the doors. At last, one that was free. She locked the door and leaned against it.

She would have to go down in a moment. She would have to tell the Head about the letter. Everyone would be disappointed. She was leaving school in two days. She had hoped to leave on a high note, not like this. Suddenly she began to vomit violently. She retched it all up, almost kneeling on the lino, her hand clutching the pages of old newspaper which hung on the hook by the side of the bowl for used STs. Then she flushed it all away and leaned against the door, feeling unable to stand. She cried then unrestrainedly. It was a long time since she had cried.

'Well. I'm not sure what we're going to do with you,' Matron said to her two days later, coming into the Sick Bay with a tray. 'Do you think you can eat anything this morning? I've brought you some tea and toast.'

◆

'Tea, please, Matron', Rachel said. She had not been sick now for twenty-four hours and she sat up feeling light-headed, but herself. She had not been in Sick Bay for years but it still smelled as it always did, disinfectant mingled with something else, the smell of stale food which made her gag a little. Matron's white uniform rustled as she walked. She felt Rachel's head with a cool hand.

'I'm not sure what we're going to do with you,' Matron repeated. 'It's Christmas. The School Buildings are closing today. Everyone else has gone home.'

'Everyone? What about my sisters?'

'Yes. They went this morning. Their tickets were booked and your aunt is expecting them. They wanted to come and see you but, of course, only sick girls are allowed in the Sick Bay. Besides they might have caught what you have and been ill over Christmas. You wouldn't have wanted that.'

'No, Matron.'

'The doctor says you're not fit to travel by train yet. Does your guardian or any of your relatives have a car? Could anyone come and collect you?'

'No, Matron.' It was not strictly true. Auntie F did have a car, but she couldn't possibly drive down from Northumberland. It would take hours, days. And then they would have to go back, and what about her sisters travelling up to Newcastle? She hoped they would manage without her, the organising elder sister, who always looked after the tickets. 'They'll be fine,' she thought to herself. But how would she be without them? She could feel the bile rising.

'No, Matron,' she said again.

'Well, I'll have to make some arrangements. Can you get yourself dressed? I'll be back soon.'

Rachel fumbled into her clothes. She felt disconnected from herself. Her arms and legs were heavy. She sat down on the bed, exhausted, and drank the now cold tea. She tried to eat the toast but it was leathery and stuck in her throat.

Her last day at school. She had imagined it so differently. She hadn't said goodbye to anyone. Would she ever see any of them again, her friends, the teachers? She would have to write and tell her parents about Oxford. She felt her eyes fill.

After what seemed like hours Matron came back. She had taken off her white uniform and she looked, Rachel realised, quite young, even pretty. 'Miss Mitchell has said you can go and stay with her and her friend, Miss Dunne, until you are well enough to travel.'

'What! Our Miss Mitchell? Micky?' She was the biology teacher, the deputy head. Everyone respected her but also feared her a little. She was stern but fair, had no favourites. But going to stay with her? Rachel felt her throat contract.

'Yes. She's coming to collect you in her car. Here's your bag. Your sister has packed your trunk and it's gone to the station with the others. I hope she got everything because you're leaving school, aren't you? I have to go and catch my train now but Miss Michell will be here soon. You'll be all right by yourself for a while, won't you?'

'Yes, Matron.'

'Here. Put this blanket round you. The central heating has been switched off and it's cold outside. Goodbye, then. I hope you manage to get home for Christmas. Good luck for 1957!'

1957! Rachel couldn't believe it. Nearly the end of the 1950s.

'Good bye, Matron.'

Matron's footsteps died away. Rachel felt the whole school around her, settling into silence. A radiator creaked. She cried now, out of weakness, out of a sense of desolation she could not name. She ought to pack her things. She scrabbled in the bedside locker for her washbag and put her hand on a slim paperback, her copy of T. S. Eliot's *Selected Poems*. It was a white and blue Penguin and had cost her one shilling and sixpence, a lot of money from the ten shillings she had each term. She must not leave this behind. She suddenly remembered something and began turning the pages looking for the words she wanted. Something like: 'This is the way the world ends, Not with a bang but a whimper.'

She shivered and gave up. She would find it later. It was definitely getting colder. She pulled the blanket round herself and waited.

THE CHILDREN'S HOME

Date: 10 October 2010
Subject: Italian Greetings
Dear Peggy,
Thanks for email. Glad you're OK.
I hope the postcard I sent from Rome arrived. Just thought I'd remind you of the holiday we had together that year after we'd both left school. I kept thinking about it when I was in Rome last week.

One of the differences between then and now was that this time I could walk about without being constantly harassed by young men. We only had a day in Rome last week so we took a tour bus of the city. As we drove past the Forum, I suddenly remembered how you and I had eventually given up trying to see the Forum because we couldn't get rid of those young men who kept following us around, putting their arms round our waists and trying to get up our skirts. I suppose two naïve, just-out-of-school English girls on their own were an obvious target and it was 1957. We just gave up and went somewhere else. We didn't feel we could do anything. It was just how things were. Now that I am grey and wrinkled, I am invisible. (Sometimes that makes me furious; sometimes I really enjoy it! Is it the same with you?) I don't know what would happen to two young women going around on their own in Rome now. They would probably be a bit more street-wise than we were, though I think we managed pretty well and we did enjoy ourselves, didn't we?

Remember sitting under a trellis and drinking coffee in the sunshine at that youth hostel in Fiesole outside Florence? Someone had told us it had belonged to Mussolini's' mistress and my memory is of rather grim dormitories, smelly hole-in-the-floor toilets along with marble floors and that terrace with views of hills and cypress trees like a Renaissance painting. I think we both felt very grown up and very pleased with ourselves that we had earned enough to get to Italy and we hadn't gone straight to University as we were supposed to. I suppose we were inventing our own 'gap year'. What trend-setters we were! I began to feel glad I had refused to stay on at school for a whole year after doing the Oxford entry. It was the first time I had not done what was expected of me!

We sat there drinking coffee and reading guide books and you said, 'It was even worth working in the Sharp's toffee factory to get here!' (You put me off toffees for life, you know.) And I said something like, 'Well, they did at least pay you better than they paid me in that Children's Home.' It's funny. You talked to me a lot about the factory but I don't think I talked about the children's home, did I?

Won't rabbit on any more. I'll be home now apart from going down south to look after my lovely granddaughter next week. Be in touch. I think of you oftener than I get round to writing!

Love,
Rachel

Rachel's Journal
12 October
Feel I'm properly back home now and sorted after the Italian trip. Garden wild and I have had lots of catching up to do. Writing to Peggy about that Italian holiday stirred up a lot for me.

I have never talked to anyone about that children's home where I worked after leaving school. Looking back, I feel that I went through that time like a sleepwalker – but it was only six or seven months from leaving school until we went to Italy in July – or was it August?

Oh! That children's home! Perhaps my situation was a bit too close to the children's. It's strange. I never thought of myself as homeless but, of course, I was. So I went to work in a 'home' for homeless children, or children whose parents had given them up or who had them taken away for various reasons. I suppose because I wasn't working class I thought that it was quite different.

The only advantage of that place was that I couldn't spend any money stuck in a village in Sussex. And I got board and lodge – that tiny bedroom at the top of the house that I shared with the silent young woman who snored, and dinners like we'd had at school. Days off were worse than working ones. I didn't have anywhere to go so I'd retreat to the local bookshop. The woman who ran the shop

*must have realized I was standing in the corner reading as much
as I could before I had to put down cash for a Penguin but she
never said anything. Amazing, now I think about it, that there was
quite a good little bookshop in such a small place. No Amazon or
Waterstone's then to squeeze the little book shops.*

Rachel paused in her writing. Was it Auntie N who had suggested
the job in a London County Council Children's home? Rachel
had thought it would be great to be in London. Didn't realize she
would be out in the depths of rural Sussex with a train every two
hours, weekdays only. She had put away the memory, shut the
door on it, but now she began to wonder about the children. What
happened to them and how strange to think they'd all be middle-aged
or grey now – those that had survived. Even then she had thought it
was a poor way to deal with kids from 'bad families' – taking them
away from London and dumping them in the middle of the Sussex
countryside. The idea must have been to get them as far from their
dreadful families as possible, make it really hard for parents to visit.
Very few did, especially as trains didn't run on Sundays. That pale
little toddler called June – her mother did get there some Saturdays,
a thin, red-haired young woman who sat hugging her daughter
and crying. The staff looked away. What could we do? Or were we
just hardened to it? Like prison guards. I liked little June. I used
to sing 'June is bustin' out all over' to her, which was one of those
songs they were endlessly playing on the 'wireless' that spring, quite
inappropriate, as she never showed much sign of bustin' out. Not
like some of the other kids, who were labelled trouble makers before
they were five and got sent on to some other institution. Poor kids!

Date: 2 November 2010
Subject: Various
Dear Peggy,
Glad the post card from Rome arrived and very glad you remembered
the young men in the Forum. I'm never entirely sure that I haven't
made up some of these memories. Writing to you about the
Children's Home brought back all sorts of things about that time
between leaving school and going to University which I had forgotten!
   You are right. I did get into Oxford (at the second attempt) while

THE CHILDREN'S HOME

I was working in the Home. You know I failed the exam I took from school. Then I was ill and couldn't travel but I was rescued by Mickey, Miss Mitchell, do you remember her? How could you forget her? We thought she was so strict, didn't we? Biology lessons, 'Bodge', but she was a brilliant teacher and we must have known she wasn't all steel because we wrote that musical for our Sixth Form end of year play where you played the singing dogfish who had escaped from her biology lab and wanted to be a pop star. I wrote that riff on the negro spiritual 'dem bones, dem bones, dem – uh – dry bones' and she loved it. So we must have known she was a softie really. (Do you remember the cheers at the end of the play when you started to sing a version of Tommy Steele's 'Singing the Blues'?)

Anyway, Mickey was so lovely to me that time; she took me out of school and nursed me on a camp bed in her living room for a couple of days until I was well enough to go up north for Christmas. I feel bad now that I never really thanked her properly. She lived with Miss D, remember her? I always thought she was *really* scary but then I was useless in her needlework classes. But she was quite sweet to me, too. I wonder now whether they were lovers, but at the time it simply did not occur to me.

So – yes – I did get into Oxford. That was thanks to my dear Auntie Chuni one of my mother's older sisters. Chuni (she was really Norah; Chuni was an Indian nickname) had been sent back from India when she was two to go to – yes – our old school. She'd been a teacher and a head mistress and told me that there was this women's college called St Anne's that did its exams in January. So, why didn't I try for it? I could delay going to work at the Home for a week or two. So that is what I did. I slept on her settee for a couple of nights, and did the exams as an external candidate. Then went off to the children's home and got called for interview while I was there. I owe Auntie Chuni a lot – more than I ever told her. But I think that was the thing with our aunts. They were just there. Like the weather.

I suppose weather will be hotting up with you. Here it is grey and chilly. Anyway, won't moan. I had a lovely time down in Devon looking after M who is utterly delightful (unprejudiced view!). How are yours?

Love, R

Rachel turned off the laptop and went to get her walking gear. She and Amy were going out into Derbyshire to climb Kinder Scout, the peak, then back for a concert at the Bridgewater Hall. As she went she thought about that network of older women – aunts, teachers – who had stretched out a safety net for her in that year. A bit late now for gratitude. You can't write thank you letters to the dead. 'The souls of the righteous are in the hand of God.' The words came into her mind but wouldn't Chuni have laughed at being described as 'a righteous soul'. She was the most Irish, the wittiest of the aunts. She'd kissed the Blarney Stone and would tell about how you had to hang upside down 'with a man holding your ankles and your skirt over your head for all to see'. But, Rachel thought, Chuni had probably always had the gift of blarney, standing on the hearth rug smoking her after dinner cigarette and holding forth. So sad when her mind failed, as it did when she was in her late sixties.

Rachel tried to remember that interview at St Anne's for which she had not worn either a suit or a hat. She had felt that somehow everyone must smell dirty nappies and sick when she went near them. She walked around in a fog of baby smells. Discussing T. S. Eliot and Dr Johnson had felt unreal. She had told no one where she was going. There was no one to tell. She had been so grateful that the interview just happened to fall on of those rare occasions during her time in the children's home when she had two days off together. She could not possibly have asked for the schedules to be changed so she could go for an interview at University.

To the other girls working there (they were all girls, mostly in their teens) going to University was not just unimaginable, it was undesirable. Rachel was already an oddity because she was so reticent about her boyfriend (the one she had rapidly invented and decided was doing his National Service). Age and gender united, class divided us, Rachel thought. I suppose I knew I was middle-class (my 'good education') but it was only later I really understood something about class and children's homes and boarding school and a ' good education'.

She had at first found the constant cursing difficult to get her mouth around – swearing at the children was just part of the currency of exchange. She learned the latest songs soon enough since 'the wireless' was constantly on. Anyway, she and Peggy had got into Johnny Ray and Tommy Steele in that last year (pop not invented yet, of course, nor the idea of being 'a teenager').

When the letter arrived from Oxford offering her a place, she was at breakfast with the other girls, the usual swearing at the toaster going on and the wireless blaring 'Magic moments, when two hearts are beating!' as it had incessantly that spring. Rachel had been exhausted from a night 'on lates', when you stood on the landing doing the ironing and making sure children did not get out of bed. Then at 9.00 p.m. you put thirty sleeping children on the potty in turn, changing wet bedding and pushing floppy limbs into dry pyjamas. Looking back, she hoped she had never slapped them or given them a bit of a shake when they got out of bed or wet themselves yet again, but she knew she had come close to it once or twice. She thought some of the other girls did give the odd impatient slap. There was one little boy called Bernard who was already labelled a troublemaker – poor kid, not yet five.

Rachel remembered opening the letter from St Anne's and thinking, 'Oh. Good!' in a dull way before putting it back in the envelope and clearing the table and going through to the toddler room. She didn't tell anyone. She didn't even write back. She got a letter a week later asking if she intended to take up the place. This jolted her and she had written back at once to say 'yes' and then she had written to Mum and Dad. She still wrote to them on her day off when she had time to go out to the Post Office and buy an airmail form and stamps. She must have written to Miss B at school as well, for a week or two later (it came back to her now) she got a very angry letter from Mrs Moore, a teacher who had given her a few extra lessons in that last term, saying that she had heard Rachel had got into Oxford and why hadn't she written to tell Mrs Moore. It had never occurred to Rachel that Mrs Moore might want to know, but she couldn't explain her lethargy to herself, let alone to anyone else. She had written back, saying she was sorry, that she had written but had forgotten to post the letter – which was a lie.

It seemed she had become an automaton, who got up, ate, looked after children during the long days, and then eventually fell into a dreamless sleep in the iron bedstead under the sloping eaves where even she, five foot nothing, was liable to bump her head. That narrow room at the top of the Home must have been the maids' room when the grand house had been privately owned, but Rachel only realized that now. She was never alone and always alone.

Every week was the same. It was with a shock one day when she realized that it was Easter Sunday. Was it church bells she had heard? She did not have a day off, but thought of Chris and Jane who would have made the journey north without her and would be sitting down to after-church roast lamb with Auntie May. Chris would be the 'big sister' now, taking charge of the tickets for the journeys she made with Jane. Chris was the rising star, resisting going to University because she wanted to be a nurse (and also because she wanted to escape from the shadow cast by her elder sister, as she told Rachel years later). Had Rachel ever written to her during those months? Probably not. She couldn't remember. Was this the moment when they had begun to drift apart, or had that already begun?

Eventually she got a letter back from India saying 'Well done!', but it was only when she had left the Home and gone out to Italy with Peggy that she had begun to realize what it meant, that letter. But of course, she didn't realize it at all – you never did.

And now she was thinking about Chris and how it was that, once they had both left school, Chris had disappeared into another life from which occasionally she emerged at family gatherings, stayed for a short time and left before anyone else. But I got caught up in my life, Rachel thought, as she went to find her climbing boots; falling in and out of love, getting married, having children, work, friendships, politics, getting unmarried, grandchildren, all that tangle in which memory could not now distinguish the threads, and Chris was always hard to pin down, you never knew where she was, what she was doing. She never got married, never had children – Chris who had always said she was going to have fourteen of them. I didn't even know she'd had an abortion until years afterwards, when she mentioned it in passing, as if I had always known, Rachel thought. Never met the men in her life, didn't know where she was living half the time, at least until she got that flat in London. She was always elusive. But then I didn't try to find her, did I? 'Sisterhood is powerful' we said back then, but somehow it wasn't powerful enough. I heard news of her from Mum and Dad, of course, once they were back in Britain. They kept in touch. Not by letter now but phone. If the landline rang on Sunday evening she still thought for half a second before she picked up the receiver, 'That will be Dad'.

VIII

DAD
(1909–98)

GOD AND LOT'S WIFE

Rachel's dream was still with her as she drank her morning cup of tea – not the details, they had vanished, but the feeling of being safe, of being held. When she woke she had felt for a moment that she was back in her childhood bed on the upstairs veranda. Even with her eyes closed she knew the mosquito net surrounded her, keeping out insects and filtering the soft darkness through its meshes. She had lain for a moment half awake and thought she could hear her father's voice, singing as he accompanied himself on the big piano downstairs, 'Unde Musik', thou heavenly art ...

It must be the letter from his publisher that had triggered the dream. She could not remember when she had last dreamed about him. He had been dead for years now. Of course, he was there in her memory like background music, but then it wasn't that different from when he was alive. He had been an absent presence through so much of her life. 'A bit like God', she thought.

'Our Father ...' She supposed she had always confused him with God in her childhood. It was not just that he preached and went about in a white cassock, but that he was the most important person in her world. He represented authority. But it was not an authority born of fear. He was her Daddy, who would take her on his knee and read to her. He sang her those songs she now sang to her grandchildren, not nursery rhymes but the versions of English folk songs he had learned in his youth, with their haunting tunes and nonsense choruses, 'Oopsie diddley dandy dee'.

When Sammy the tortoise had got lost, Daddy was the one who helped her look for him, searching the scrubby grass of the compound. They never found Sammy. Perhaps he'd walked in his steady tortoise way into the shola at the back of the compound where there were snakes and Rachel was not allowed to go. She had sobbed and would not be consoled. But he had told her that tortoises were very good at looking after themselves. They couldn't really be lost because they always had their house with them and anyway God would look after him. Perhaps Sammy had made friends with the snakes and they were all happy together in the shola. 'For they shall not hurt or destroy in all my holy mountain.'

How old was she then? Five? Four? Already she was used to the way he came and went from her life. When he was there the bungalow was full of people, going in and out of the office, loud conversations in Tamil on the veranda, boring conversation with visitors at lunch time. If he was there, sometimes after lunch he would go to the big black piano, lift the lid and say 'Only for a moment' as he sat down to play. The story of the compensation piano was retold to many visitors over the table at meal times.

She liked it best when there were no visitors. Then sometimes after they had eaten, he would sit at the piano and begin to play and sing while she and Chrissie leaned against the piano stool. 'Oh! the oak and the ash and the bonny rowan tree, they flourish at home in my own country.'

Someone had sent him the music for the songs from the Disney film of *Snow White and the Seven Dwarfs*, so, years before they had ever seen a film, they knew all the songs by heart.

'What about "Some Day my prince will come"?' He turned the cheap paper pages.

'No. Play, "I like to dance and tap my feet",' they would say and then they'd sing as loudly as they could, dancing round and stamping their feet, being dwarves.

'That's all now. Bye bye, my dears,' Daddy would put down the piano lid, give them a quick kiss. Then he would disappear 'to the villages' for several days and come back with stories which she half-heard, half-understood, of walking through the paddy fields, preaching and then sleeping under the stars, sorting out quarrels, dealing with the budmash, baptisms. His coming and going had been the rhythm of her early childhood.

God was always there but you couldn't see him. Perhaps he was always in the villages.

Once Chrissie was frightened because the Sunday School teacher told her that God had a big eye and a big ear and could see everything you did and hear everything you said. Chrissie kept looking for God's big eye in the sky and one night she cried and cried because she didn't want God to keep looking at her. Mummy said, 'That Sunday school teacher is a silly woman. God isn't like that.' Chrissie was little and she was scared of lots of things. Another night they were coming home in the mission car. It was a special treat for them to go in the car. They had been to the hospital to see the Baxters and it was late. Rachel and Chris sat in the back of the car and looked out of the window. It was exciting being out in the dark. The full moon was low in the sky and ran along the tops of the palm trees and over the rooftops. It kept up with them all the way. Chris was scared of the moon. 'The Boony! The Boony! It's following us,' she cried and slid down to hide her face in the seat. Rachel was too big to be frightened of the moon but she knelt beside Chris in the back of the car and they pressed their faces into the car seat which smelled of leather and dust.

Every night Mummy said prayers with them. Rachel and Chris would shut their eyes and put their hands together. 'Thank you God for food and clothes and everything. God bless Mummy and Daddy and the aunties and uncles. Amen.' Then they would sing a verse of a hymn, 'Now the day is over' or 'When he com-eth, when he com-eth to make up his jew-els.' Their favourite was 'God who made the earth'. They sang the verse and then sang 'A-Amen' and Mummy would kiss them good night and tuck the mosquito net in carefully to make sure all the insects were kept out. 'Amen' was a funny word. Rachel liked saying it. You said it at the end of prayers and sang it at the end of hymns. Ah-men.

On Sundays Mummy and Rachel and Chris would put on their best dresses and walk to church across the compound. The tailor had made Rachel and Chrissie the same dress except that Rachel's was blue and Chrissie's was green. They sat on the women's side with all the ladies in their beautiful saris. Rachel loved the colours of the saris – red, turquoise, and blue, with gold edges. They rustled and shone in the sunshine coming through the open doors. The air was sweet with the jasmine all the ladies had in their hair. Mummy never wore jasmine, though sometimes if they went out somewhere special she and Daddy came home with the garlands that had been put round their necks. Rachel thought when she was grown up she would have long dark hair and wear it wound up at the back with jasmine in it.

The men mostly wore white shirts and dhotis or darker trousers, so their side of church was boring.

Rachel and Chris liked the hymns. They stood on the bench on each side of Mummy and pretended to read out of the hymn books, and tried to sing. Mostly they didn't know the hymns but once the preacher announced that it was 'God who made the earth.' Rachel and Chris sang the verse and the 'Amen' as loud as they could. But there was another verse, one they didn't know. They did know to sing 'Amen' at the end. But nobody else did. At the end of the next verse they sang 'A-Amen' again but still it wasn't the end. They began to giggle. 'Don't sing Amen until I tell you', Mummy whispered to them. When she said 'All right', they all three sang 'A-amen' but the piano man didn't play it and no one else sang it. Mummy went very red in the face and tried not to giggle, too, as they sat down. Rachel and Chris snuggled up one on each side of her for the boring bit of the service. On the way home one of the Aunties who lived in the other house on the compound met them and said something to Mummy which made her go red in a different way. Daddy said that those Aunties thought children should be seen and not heard.

It was not his philosophy. His children were all chatterboxes, but how could they not be when their childhood was awash with words. They splashed around in them. They all talked at once. Words! All those silly rhymes and limericks which he loved, versions of Bible sayings, jokes half-understood. Rachel smiled as she remembered. Yesterday she had found that, yet again, she had lost her umbrella and had walked down the road through the puddles saying under her breath,

> *The rain it raineth on the just*
> *and also on the unjust fella,*
> *But more upon the just*
> *because the unjust has the just's umbrella.*

Oh and the limericks! How Dad loved limericks, both his own – made up 'at the drop of a hat' or rather at the drop of an odd place name or strange word and those which embodied a particular kind of clerical humour.

GOD AND LOT'S WIFE

There once was a fellow called Sam
Said, Isn't it strange that I am
Just a creature that moves
In predestinate grooves
Not a bus, not a bus, but a tram.

Take-offs of familiar hymns like 'Sit down, Oh, Men of God!' sung loudly to the tune of 'Rise up, Oh, Men of God'.

When he left India the first time, believing that an Indian should have his job, he became what he called an Ecclesiastical brass-hat, a bureaucrat who shuttled between Geneva, London and New York. He missed the villages. (Of course, he would go back when invited.) He sat in committee meetings making up limericks about those around the table – affectionate limericks about senior church leaders. And in his old age when he could not sleep he lay in bed and composed limericks based on the names of all the places Paul had visited in his missionary journeys. 'There was an old man of Thermopolae ...'

Paul was his great hero. For of course above and in the centre of all the swirling, tumbling, words, he had believed there was The Word, The Gospel, the Good News. Rachel still had the copy of the Bible he had given her when she left University. He favoured the Revised Standard Version. She still kept it by her bed with its red worn covers and his inscription in the front in his illegible hand, 'Love from Daddy. Psalm 121 verse 8. The Lord will keep thy going out and thy coming in from this time forth for ever more.' Going out and coming in. Coming and going. With his battered leather case and his beloved portable typewriter. Rachel thought of the way he would sit down anywhere, his typewriter on his knees and bash away at the keys. In his old age, as he got increasingly blind, his typing became more and more erratic but he kept on writing, writing and speaking, and traveling to conferences to speak up for what he knew was right.

Such confidence! 'Proper confidence' he had talked about, but what about uncertainty, hesitancy, the not being sure you were right? Were these proper to the daughters? The inheritance of femininity? And what about that other inheritance, his literary legacy, the physical reminder of those hours he spent at the typewriter – mostly in his old age. She always put off dealing with the letters when they came, stuffed them into a file until she felt able to deal with them. Today she really must get on and answer the publisher's letter. It wasn't just his ghost who was present to her. It was those files of correspondence and the occasional emails from those who wanted to keep his books in print, or wanted somehow to claim a piece of him. 'I am writing a thesis on your father. Could you please answer some questions about his style of preaching and would you be prepared to answer some questions about your relationships to him as a daughter?' She had come to dread the emails headed 'Your Father'.

He was, of course, a patriarch.

Was that why she had become a feminist? Neither of her sisters had, but Chrissie had been furious with him. She had raged at the absences, the being abandoned, the sense that she, they, were not as important as those others, known and unknown who claimed his time, attention, and – yes – his love. Perhaps she was angry because Rachel couldn't be. Perhaps she carried Rachel's hurt and rage. Hadn't R. D. Laing said that was what happened in families? Rachel tried to recall those discussions they had had in the 70s when they were reading Laing and everything seemed open to change – politics, work, the family. Ah! The family! How her women's group had argued over it all; patriarchy, fatherhood, the contradictions of their lives. They all adored their fathers. They all hated their fathers. They loved men. They loved women. They were furious with men. They were furious with other women – especially their mothers.

'But I do think patriarchy is a useful concept.'

'Well, my Dad was ruled by my Mum. What she said went.'

'It's about structural inequality. Not necessarily individual fathers but about how men are always privileged as against women.'

'My Mum gave up her job when she got married, even though she'd had been senior to my Dad and then she has had to rely on him for money all her life.'

'Yes. I had another row with my Mum last time she came to visit. She does everything for my Dad – everything – and, of course, my brother can do no wrong as far as she's concerned.'

'But look at you – you're as bad as me. We gave up our jobs to look after the babies and our husbands are earning the money and leaving us to do everything. You're always saying how much you hate housework. But you do it and you always have to be the one to make arrangements about the children. New men! Show me one.'

Rachel could never speak about her own father in the group. She had never mentioned her own childhood. She was involved in political activity, the peace movement, the Labour Party. She did a post-graduate degree, working in the evenings when the children were asleep. She got a job lecturing. Was that the nearest she could get to having a pulpit to preach from? She had never thought of it like that. She had discussed the job in the group.

'This new job I've got at the Poly ...'

'Yes. You're the only woman in the Department, I hear.'

'Well, the only academic. The others are all men. But the secretaries and clerical staff are all women – and the cleaners – of course.'

'So, it's all about gender.'

'Class and gender. The porters are all men and get paid more than the cleaners – I hear – and I get paid more than the porters.'

'So?'

'I was thinking I might try and put some stuff about women into the syllabus. Offer a lecture on women. Yes, and we need a nursery.'

'A lecture on Patriarchy! That's what they need!'

'Dump a load of dirty washing on their desks. That's what they need!' They all laughed – but ruefully. They knew none of them would do such a thing.

She'd stopped going to church by then, walked out when the local vicar gave a speech attacking trades unions, though she had gone back to tell him why she was leaving. All those women wanting to be priests in the Church of England. She couldn't understand it. 'Sweep the whole thing away!' she thought. Have done with it. But at work she tried to be polite, well-behaved, avoid confrontation except when she had to. She was shocked when she was greeted on the stairs by a senior member of the Polytechnic with the words, 'How are the nutty feminists then?' She had met him only once since answering some question from him at her interview. Was it because she never wore a bra? Or because she had argued in a staff committee for a nursery? Or that some of her colleagues drank with him in the pub after work and exchanged stories?

She had gone home, as usual, picked up the two children from her neighbour who looked after them three days a week and then she had cooked tea for her husband and the children, before putting them to bed and settling down to her own preparation for the next day. She never had much sleep in those years.

Her parents were busy with their second and last departure from India and their letters were full of farewell 'dos' and plans for their journey home overland. Her father did not mention the fact that she had gone back to work full-time. Her mother asked who was looking after the children and how Peter was coping. Rachel's elder daughter who was nearly five had asked, 'Why don't we have a nana like Anthony and Hazel?'

'You do have a nana and grandpa but they live a long way away', Rachel had tried to explain. 'You'll see them soon.'

'Tracey's nana lives in Hull and she goes to see her.'

'Yes, I know, darling. But India is further away than Hull. You will see them when you are a bit older.'

Later, when Mum and Dad had 'retired' (not that he ever was) and settled in Birmingham, she had tried to talk to them about their absence for all those years of her growing up, about boarding school and about the deserts of the holidays, when – she felt now – they had stumbled about in a sort of half-light, broken by brief electric flashes of activity and joy, when he came home for a couple of days on the way from some conference in Geneva. It had happened perhaps twice or three times in all those years but they were lit up in her memory. He had arrived like a hero come to make sure of the happy ending but of course, it was not the end of the story and when he disappeared again two days later, everything sunk back again into greyness. But she had never been able to say that to them. The weekly letters were always up-beat, Pravda-style, as her brother joked in later years. She still wanted his approval, still wanted to be Daddy's girl.

Talking about it in that Birmingham room with its Indian picture and the line of painted elephants on the mantel piece was difficult. Mum just repeated like a mantra, 'I was very happy at school. Very happy.' But Rachel thought he had listened. When he preached the sermon on the fiftieth anniversary of his ordination, he had apologized from the pulpit to his family who, he said, had borne the burden of his ministry. She was moved and grateful to him but the public event was not the conversation she wanted. She argued with him in her head but it was hard to do when he was there. And he was not there a great deal. He was still very busy, even in retirement he was writing, preaching, taking on a church in a run-down bit of Birmingham that everyone else thought ought to be closed.

He was a father to a lot of people. Everyone wanted a piece of him and sometimes there wasn't much left for his daughters.

God was a jealous God.

Rachel thought of him the last time she had seen him in the hospital bed with an oxygen mask and the clatter of the ward around him. He had not thought he would die before Mum.

'My will,' he gasped. 'In the top drawer of the desk. I've left everything to Mum.'

'Yes, of course, Dad. We'll see to it. Try to rest.'

'I haven't done anything about my literary estate. I had thought…' he put the oxygen mask back on and took a breath, 'Will you do it?'

'Yes, Dad, of course. Don't worry about it.'

'Can you get my Psalm tape out of the cupboard?' Rachel had scrabbled about in his hospital locker and found the tape which he had played daily since becoming too blind to read. She laid it by his hand on the bed. She tried to hold his hand. When had she last done that? But he was restless. 'It's dark,' he said. 'I keep singing, "Lead kindly light amid the encircling gloom", to myself, of course.'

'Yes, though not sure anyone would notice here if you stood up and sang an aria,' Rachel said, glaring at the nurses who were talking loudly in the 'station' next to his bed. The ward was a noisy place, full of clatter and chatter.

'No breath,' he smiled.

She thought of the words of the night prayer. 'Grant us a quiet night and a perfect end.'

'Dad,' she wanted to say, 'Don't die.' She wanted to say, 'I know you're old and have had a good life but there is so much I want to say that I haven't said.' She wanted to say, 'I love you, Dad. But why haven't we really talked to each other properly for so long? Ever since – well – ever since I went to boarding school?' but a man dressed in clerical black appeared by the bed. She did not recognize him.

'I've come down from Birmingham to see you', he said over her head. 'Do you remember me?'

He looked doubtful but then smiled 'Of course', through the oxygen mask. 'This is my daughter.'

The man nodded and sat down, ignoring her. She struggled with tears of rage and sorrow, but rage at whom? The stranger or her father? God, perhaps. She had left then with the words unspoken, whatever they were.

She hadn't come back. He died that night with someone else sitting by his bed, someone she did not know.

But she had all his music, bound in cheap cardboard in the bazaar, and she would get it out and play it sometimes, turning the crumbling pages carefully. 'Thou Heavenly art, in many hours of darkness.' His sayings and songs rose to her lips with her grandchildren as they had with her children. 'Oopsie diddley dandy dee.'

And she had inherited from him her love of the hills, her delight in wild places. She remembered that last summer (though, of course, they had not known it was his last). She had taken both Mum and Dad for 'a little holiday' in Northumberland. She'd booked them into a B and B. One late afternoon, they had left Mum resting and taken the track up onto the moors behind 'Granny's house', where they had spent so many summers. He was nearly blind but walked confidently with his stick along the familiar track, only occasionally stumbling a little on rough ground. It was early September. The heather was just over, but the hills were still dark purple and smelled honey-sweet. There were bronze glints in the bracken. The valley below them was green in the late afternoon sun which caught the meanders of the river. Above and beyond rose the 'frog's eyes' of Simonside. She saw it all as he could not. They walked in companionable silence to 'The Climbing Rock', where he and his sisters had practised their early rock climbing moves.

'You know,' he said as they paused before turning to make their way down the slope, 'when I went to work with the unemployed miners in Wales when I was a student in the 30s, I remember talking to one of the men and he said, "This valley will be in my heart, where ever I go". I thought the valley didn't look that special and it was a rather sentimental thing to say but that is what I feel about this place. This valley. These hills. They've always been in my heart. I can see them clearly still.'

It was where they scattered his ashes. It was how she liked to remember him, walking across the moors with his stick in his hand.

◆

Remember Lot's wife! The family joke always repeated if you were on a walk and someone dropped behind to 'pay a visit' as her mother said. How old was she when she eventually read the Bible story of how Lot's wife was turned into a pillar of salt because she looked back? Of course, Rachel had tried to read the whole Bible through when she was what? –nine or ten. It was about the time she learned the order of the books by heart. She still remembered them, could rattle them off, major and minor prophets – Amos, Obadiah, Jonah, Micah …

Remember Lot's wife! Perhaps that was what has happened to me, she thought. It is dangerous to look back. I have become a pillar of salt, looking back at the cities of the plain – which I suppose is where I have lived. How was it that her father who struggled with racism before there was a word for the concept, who tried to think about feminism – though not with much success, how was it that in his last years he had been so taken up by the homophobic paranoia that gripped some parts of the Church? It was one of the things she had never talked to him about.

Lot was such a strange figure in that strange yet so familiar Old Testament world. Perhaps Dad was Lot offering his daughters to protect the angels, who came as strangers to the house. These were the bits of the story that all the clerical attacks on gay people forgot, that Lot was protecting the outsiders, the strangers within the gates. But also that he was offering up his daughters. These men were more important than the daughters. Were we, Dad's daughters, offered up, so that the strangers might be protected? Chrissie thought so. But, as so often, the fate of the minor female characters was not explained, their histories were unimportant. What happened to the daughters? Did Lot's wife provide a rich source of salt for passing cattle and people – after all, salt was a valuable commodity? Was it her tears which solidified and paralysed her? Perhaps that was it.

'Tears do that', Rachel thought. 'Auntie May, for example, she was Lot's wife, frozen in grief and looking back for her husband, for her dead boys, the cousins I never knew, killed in the war. My generation of women were fortunate. We did not lose our men – husbands, sons or lovers – to a war. But other things turn us to salt, perhaps. '

When she had started to go back into a church, it was to cry. She went past the door of the church on the corner one Sunday, saw it was open, and went in. The dark gothic exterior opened to reveal a surprisingly light and airy space in which a few people sat quietly waiting for the service to begin. She had sat down behind a pillar and, whether it was the mixture of long silence and familiar words or the fact that no-one knew her, she did not know, but suddenly she felt free to cry. The Greek Orthodox church, someone had told her, held that tears were a form of sacrament. Anglicans didn't, of course, but no one seemed to mind her crying quietly behind the pillar.

The service reminded her of the ones she had attended from school when Dad had decided she should be prepared for confirmation. She begged not to go to the local parish church to which they processed in crocodile each Sunday wearing those hated n-- brown hats, 'the animals went in two by two'. So she and Peggy had gone down the hill to Mr Butler's church for classes. Then once a month on Sunday mornings, the two of them would get up before anyone else in the dormitory and walk the couple of miles to go to the 8 o'clock service. She had loved those walks through quiet streets, houses with curtains drawn on imagined lives, all dreaming towards dawn. The world was theirs in that moment. After the service they went back with the Butler family, and had boiled eggs and home-made bread. She understood a little in those breakfasts of what the breaking of bread might mean.

Her breakfast now was solitary but she ate contentedly watching through the window at the sparrows jostling each other at the bird feeder. That rather clunky couplet which she had read somewhere kept coming back to her:

> *So through all eternity,*
> *I forgive you, you forgive me.*

till in the end she went to look it up.

GOD AND LOT'S WIFE

The internet is a wonderful thing. She found it straight away. It was the last verse of one of Blake's strange poems, 'Broken Love'.

And throughout all Eternity
I forgive you, you forgive me.
As our dear Redeemer said:
'This the Wine, and this the Bread.'

She sat a moment, her father vivid to her as on that last walk in his beloved hills when they had not needed many words.

Then, she drew the laptop to her again and began to write to her sister.

Manchester Dec. 1st
Dear Jane,
I've had Dad's American publisher in touch with me. I enclose copies of letters. Hope you think this is OK. I am writing to James as well. Strange to think that if Dad had been alive he would have been 101 this month! I remember once when I was about nine telling him that he had the same birthday as Mary Queen of Scots! And he was suitably impressed. Will ring.
    Love,
    Rachel

IX

MANY WATERS
(1970, 2005)

AUNTIES

Rachel was sitting at the kitchen table. She loved her kitchen. She had chosen to paint the end wall bright red to set off the grey tiles and wooden cupboards and now she sat, the letters spread out on the table, enjoying the colour – and also the warmth from the kitchen radiator. She had just come back from visiting her family in Bristol. It was lovely to have that time with them and to see the children but she was glad to be home, to sit in her own snug kitchen.

Today she had decided to start on the project of sorting out old letters and papers. One of the things Dad and Mum had done so gracefully was to shed their possessions, so that when they died Rachel, as their executor, did not have to go through whole households of stuff deciding what to keep. Rachel had done that for Auntie Faith after her death. Oh – the papers! There were even some of her sixth form essays in an old book box under the stairs. No, Rachel thought, she must start to clear things so that when she died her children were spared that. The cabin trunk under the spare room bed felt too daunting so she was beginning on the drawers in the old desk.

A bundle of old letters from the 1970s and 1980s lay on the table, including some she had grabbed up from Chris's flat when they were going through it after her death. She began to turn them over when she recognised her own hand-writing. Chris had kept some of her letters! They were held together by a large paper clip. She started to read.

Feb. 15th, 1970
Dear Chris,
I know you have moved up to Nottingham but I don't have an address for you, so am sending this to your old address and hope it gets forwarded. Can you let me know if you get it? Hope you're OK. I am not clear what kind of a community it is you have joined, so write and tell me about it, or better still, come and visit.

We are all OK though I am still not getting much sleep. However, the baby is fine – just hungry – and Anne is fine – chatting away now. I am finding it hard work with the two little ones and Peter out all day and a lot of evenings. Some mornings I think I am never going to get out of the house! Do come and see us. The children change so much and they'd love to see their auntie Chris! No more now but will write again when I have an address.

Lots of love, R

She put the letter to one side and thought about that time in her life when she was at home with a toddler and a small baby. She had loved it but it was hard. There was none of the support for young mothers her daughters had – NCT groups and play groups. All her friends were still working. The other young mother in her street had her mother living nearby. That's why she had decided to set up this new thing – a 'pre-school play group' with – what was her name? – that dark-haired woman down the road. They had got the vicar to agree to the use of the church hall. Rachel remembered her elder daughter in her baby walker – one of the earliest, and rather rickety but that didn't stop the baby charging up and down the bare boards of the church hall crowing with delight. Did Annie's baby look like her? Not really.

She took up the next letter. Chris had obviously arranged them in date order.

March 20th , 1970
Dearest Sis,
So glad you got my birthday letter and the book. Do tell me more about the community in Nottingham when you next write. It sounds great. Just what you were looking for. Do you have a job there? We're all well apart from a few snuffles. I am tired but OK. Peter is away in Germany so everything is full on. I am planning to get some part-time work if I can sort out child-care. Will tell you all but DO come and see us. Or, you know we have a phone now. I think I sent out the number with the Christmas card but let me know if you don't have it. Do you have a phone there?

Talking of having a phone, Auntie F rang me up a few days

ago! I haven't seen her for ages, though of course we exchange Christmas cards (not presents!). I've never given her a present since that time – do you remember? – when we were in Rothbury one Christmas and neither of us had any money left for presents (I think I'd have been about fifteen) and she said we could look in the drawer where she kept a stock of things she'd been given that she didn't want and we discovered every present we had given her for the last N Christmases. I suppose bath-salts and scarves are a bit boring but we never knew what to give her, did we? She usually gave us money, I remember. And Auntie Nan gave us books.

The funny thing was that though Auntie F taught English she wasn't really interested in books, was she? Do you remember that Christmas when Auntie N had given me some book, I think it was Catcher in the Rye, which had just come out, and Auntie F told her it was a wicked novel and should be banned. Nan asked her if she had read it and she said, 'Of course not', and they had one of their rows. I think they were really fond of each other but they did argue all the time, didn't they? I used to think it was a wonder we every got out on a walk or a picnic WITH a packed lunch. (Do you remember those fish paste sandwiches?) You and I just used to keep our heads down, didn't we!

Anyway, Auntie F rang up. I thought something terrible must have happened but then it turned out she had rung to tell me that God wanted me to go to some MRA play which is on in London at the moment. You know MRA own some theatre or other – forgotten what it's called. I nearly asked her what baby-sitting arrangements God had in mind but I didn't. I did say, 'You know I have a small baby and a toddler. What do you suggest I do with them?' She said, 'Can't Peter look after them for 24 hours'. I pointed out that he had a full-time job and anyway they haven't quite worked out a way for men to breast-feed babies, though no doubt they will get round to it soon. I think I was rude to her and I felt quite upset afterwards. She really hasn't a clue but then I have no clue about her and her life, except that she is still very involved with MRA.

Hope you are OK. Do ring and DO come and visit if you can. Haven't seen you for ages.

Love, R.

Auntie F, thin, restless – no wonder really; 'absolute honesty, absolute purity, absolute unselfishness and absolute love'. These were the demands that Moral Re-Armament made of its followers, of which Auntie F must have been among the most ardent. She must have felt a constant failure. And she was – yes! She was – always embattled. Evil could pop up anywhere not just in the set books on the English syllabus but in the NUT, where she fought the Communist devil most energetically.

I suppose, Rachel thought, she became a teacher because that is what women of her class and education did, if you didn't get married. I think she hated it really. As for us coming to stay occasionally … maybe she did 'love' us, but 'like' us? I am not sure. But she and I got on better when she was old and her crippling arthritis, which might have made her more bitter and angry, somehow didn't. She found a way to live with it. I used to go and see her – after the children were grown up. She didn't enjoy small children.

Rachel's thoughts were drifting. She was remembering again that time after her second child was born and how she had walked around in a daze from lack of sleep. The baby had gone on waking up for a feed at night much longer than her elder child – or perhaps it was just having two of them so close together in age – though not as close as Chris and me, she thought. But – though she never told anyone this – she had loved the night feed. Sitting up in bed propped up by pillows, with the house in darkness, everything silent around her except for quiet breathing, she had felt a profound delight. It came back to her now as she sat in her warm kitchen. Usually she had drifted into a kind of half-sleep as the baby tugged gently at her, blissed out, falling asleep and waking suddenly to suck a little longer – just for the pleasure of it, not for the milk. 'Like a child upon its mother's breast,' Rachel found the Psalmist's image of the soul resting in God, came into her mind.

She came back to the present and thought of that daughter, now pregnant and due to give birth soon. She picked up some other letters.

March 24th ,1971
Dear Chris,
I'm not sure of your address, so sending this on spec, as Mum would say. Can you please let me know if you get it. I sent a letter to the community in Nottingham where I thought you were but it's been returned to me. I am hoping you have moved back to

London. I've written to Jane but, as you know, she has the new baby and anyway I wanted to let you know about Auntie May. I really, really, need some advice and support. Mum and Dad, haven't a clue, of course.

I think when we last spoke I had just agreed to have May to stay here for a week or so. That is weeks ago now. Her neighbour rang last night to ask how she was, you know Mrs O'Connell, the neighbour who eventually gave the police my phone number when May was brought home for the fourth or fifth time after wandering through the Huyton estates late at night without a clue how to get home or even a very clear sense of where she lived.

The Bluebell estate is not a great place to be wandering around in, even in daylight, so Mrs O was right to tell the police that May couldn't look after herself anymore and they should contact the family – and we're the family she's got now, aren't we – given that her surviving sisters are either off in India or incapacitated (Chuni's dementia is worse than May's. It must be a family thing!). Mrs Packer is a bit older than May and is down south now living with her son. I got her address and wrote to her but she wrote back saying she wished she could come and see her old friend but she can't even get up here very easily.

Poor May! She keeps asking where she is and when she can go home. Then every few minutes she says 'What's the time?' and asks if it is dinner-time. She eats well, in fact I found her downstairs raiding the fridge a couple of nights ago. (Did I tell you that we've bought a fridge?? Moving into the late twentieth century, we are. It is nice not to have milk going off and not having to shop so often.) Anyway, as I was saying about May, I have been locking the doors but even so she managed to get out a couple of times. The first time Mrs Murray in the Post Office rang me to say that May was in the shop and would I come round. I had just got back from picking up the children from my neighbour who looks after them after nursery school twice a week and had found May gone. I asked Mrs M to keep May chatting if she could while I got the children back into coats and shoes (they did not want to go out again!) but dear Mrs M had managed to keep May in the shop until I got there. After that I put a slip of paper with my phone number and address into May's coat pocket and another into her handbag, and so the next time a policeman brought her back.

But I can't keep on, Chris. It is like having another baby – only worse. Last night she nearly set herself on fire standing in front of the gas fire in the living room. I smelled scorching and managed to get there in time but who knows what will happen next. I feel so sad for her but she is driving me insane. You know how she always used to go round humming hymn tunes. She has been singing 'Oh, Hear us when we cry to thee for those in peril on the sea' until I feel like screaming. Peter is in Germany, and it is quite hard anyway on my own with the two children and work and everything.

I really don't know what to do. I can't have May here and look after her. She can't be housed here in Manchester. She will have to be housed in Liverpool but that is going to take ages and you know May has never had any money. She does have the house but a two up-two down terrace on the edge of a Liverpool overspill estate which hasn't been decorated since the early 50s isn't going to fetch anything. That built-on bit at the back with the kitchen and bathroom has been coming away from the main house for years (Do you remember how your breath used to billow out in the bathroom and the draught from the crack in the wall used to whistle round the bath?) I don't know how the whole thing hasn't fallen into the garden long ago.

I feel so sad. If anyone deserves a good ending it is May. When I think about her life I wish I could do something better for her. But what? Please give me a ring as soon as you get this. Meanwhile I am ringing the Council every day. I really can't look after her here.

Speak soon,

Love, R

Manchester

June 27th, 1971

Dear Chris,

Thanks so much for ringing. I am afraid I did go on and on about May but I was desperate. Anyway, I have now managed to get Liverpool Council to offer her a place in their 'Home' on the Bluebell Estate (why do they give names of flowers to sink estates?). At least she is in Huyton, not in some dump on the other side of Liverpool. I think her doctor put pressure on the Council, which is great.

Ironic, isn't it? May always wanted to distinguish herself from the Liverpool 'overspill', as she called it, and here she is in the middle of it.

Hope you're OK. It's such ages since we've spoken so it was great to hear you – even though we'd both have wished it was about something else.

Will be in touch,
Love, R

August 29th
Dear Chris,
Tried to ring but couldn't get you so thought I'd let you know that I have been to see Auntie May in the 'home', as they call it. (Another misnomer!) Chris, it is terrible. It really is like the workhouse. The building is quite new but it already looks grubby and stinks of you know what. May is in a room with two other women. She has a bed and a locker for her things – and that's it. Just like our cubicles at school. She was sitting on the bed when we got there. I went with her neighbour, who does want to see May but finds it difficult with her children and the fact that she has to take two buses. May was up and dressed and looked quite neat but she was very subdued and I wondered what she was on. She recognised me and as soon as I arrived, she got up and said, 'Are we going home now?' I said no, I was visiting her because she lived here now, but she really didn't take it in. She sat down and said, 'What's the time?' And then a few minutes later, 'Are we going home now?' And so it went on. The only place we could all sit was on the bed. It was awful. The worst thing was one of the other women in the room sat on her bed rocking to and fro and keening – I can't think of any other way of describing it. I felt terrible when we came away. I wish we could find her somewhere else to stay. There really isn't.

I saw one of the staff on the way out. She looked harassed and said in broad scouse that May was doing all right and the Vicar and some of the ladies from the Church had been in to see her. I asked if there was a day room and she said 'Down the corridor' but when I looked in, it was like a small doctor's waiting room with chairs round the wall. All the old women were sitting staring into space and smoking. You could hardly see across the room for smoke, so I thought May was well out of it, given that she has always said she has a weak chest. There is no garden or anything, so perhaps when I come I can take May out for a walk somewhere – not that the air is exactly fresh in that estate. I came away and had a good cry, but felt helpless. I really cannot have her to stay with me so I think I will just have to keep trying to get over to see her. It means I have to get child-care, of course. I am going go over in the next couple of weeks to sort out her house and go through her things so we can put the house on the market. Do come up if you can. I know it is a long way from London. I've written to Jane, but she's got the baby. It would be good if you could come up to see May, even though she probably won't remember. Anyway, it would be lovely to see you. It's been ages.

Love,

R.

Manchester, Dec. 14th

Dear Chris,

Sorry you haven't been able to get up to Manchester again. I am sending you in a separate package some of the photos and things which you said you wanted when we spoke. Going through May's house has been very hard but her wonderful friend, Mrs Packer, did come up for a day and went through some things with me, laughing and wheezing and crying all at the same time. Her son had brought her up and she couldn't stay very long. She looks much older but she sounds just the same as she did on those Sunday afternoons when she came round for tea. Do you remember how she and May used to sit in front of the gas fire with their skirts hitched up eating May's cakes? (How did May remain so skinny all her life? Mrs. P didn't, of course, though there is much less of her now than there used to be.)

The main thing Mrs P and I did together was go through the box of papers and photos I mentioned to you and Jane. It made me understand a lot more about May's life. First, there was her marriage certificate and a wedding photo. I realised that May never had any photos of her husband or their wedding up anywhere, did she? They were married just at the end of the First World War in early 1919. He had a handle-bar moustache and May had one of those close-fitting hats. Then there were the three birth certificates for the three boys. I hadn't realised they were so close in age – only eighteen months between Harry and Robbie and then John came three years behind. There were some photos of the whole family taken not very long after John was born. Auntie May had written the date (March 1925) on the back.

Mum once told me that May's husband died when John was just six, so he must have died in about 1931. He must have been quite young. May's never talked about him to us, has she? – well she has never talked about the past at all. But it must have been hard for her, a young widow, bringing up three boys by herself and, of course, John, the baby, was always 'delicate'. I never knew quite what was wrong with him, though Mum once did tell me that he had been premature and was a bit brain damaged. Of course, in those days they couldn't care for premature babies as they do now. I always liked him with his slow speech and his beloved dog.

There were various photos of the boys and a letter from Liverpool Grammar School saying that Harold had got a scholarship to the school and then there was one two years later saying Robert had one and lots of certificates and prizes from the school and school photos. Mum told me both the older boys were very bright. I found a photo of them all with Mum when it must have been her school holidays. I know she was proud of being an auntie when she was only twelve. May must have been twenty-eight. The boys got places at Liverpool University but the War was beginning and they both went into the army straight from school. I don't know whether they chose to go into Gurkha regiments because of the family connection with India. I wonder if I could ask May. There is so much I want to talk to her about now if it is not too late.

Mrs P had to go at this point. Her son came to collect her and take her home. She sent her love to you and Jane but I went on looking through the papers. Next there was a brown envelope with, Oh! Chris!, a telegram in it and a letter from Robbie's Commanding officer in Burma saying what a great soldier Robbie had been and how he had recommended him for decoration because he had behaved with exceptional gallantry in the face of enemy fire and how she must be proud of him. He was a few days off his twentieth birthday when he died, Chris. Nineteen! Next to it was another envelope with another telegram and a letter from Harry's officer telling her he was dead in Italy. It was 1944 and he was twenty-three. They told her they would send her back his Gurkha sword. It is strange. I always knew they had both been killed in the war but those telegrams and letters, which had obviously been opened and folded and opened and folded again and again, made them real to me, those cousins we never knew.

The most awful thing, in a way, was that there was almost nothing there about John – just a few photos, one I liked and am going to keep of him sitting in the back garden of May's old house with a cigarette in one hand and the other hand on Wendy's collar. How he loved that dog! He is smiling in that slightly lop-sided way he had and Wendy seems to be grinning at the camera too. I remember Jane telling me that she had once asked Dad what was the most difficult thing he had ever done in his life. He said the hardest thing by far was when he went to Bombay to meet the boat on which Mum and May and all of us were coming back to India after James was born. It should have been a moment of unalloyed delight. The union of the churches in South India for which he had worked so hard had been accomplished and he was one of the new bishops, helping to make it all happen, he was going to meet his wife and daughters who had been separated from him for six months. He was going to see his baby son for the first time and, for May, it was to be her holiday of a life-time. But Dad had a telegram in his hand which had just arrived and he was going to have to tell May that John had killed himself. It was the first time May had ever left John. He had been staying with friends of hers, who were caring for him. He had just celebrated his twenty-third birthday. That was May's trip to India.

I sometimes wonder if Mum and Dad asked May to be our guardian as a sort of compensation for having lost her own children. But, we couldn't be, could we?

I'm writing to Jane and sending her some photos too. Will let you know when I next go to visit May.

Much love,
Rachel

Rachel put the letters back into the brown envelope. That evening she rang Jane.

'D'you know what happened to the photos of Harry and Robbie and Robbie's medals and the Ghurkha knife – all the things that Auntie May kept on that little table in her front room?' she asked her sister. 'I know Mum and Dad had them in the house in Birmingham when they came back from India but I don't remember seeing them when they were in the Home in London.'

'Don't know about the photos but Dad gave away the medals and the Gurkha knife,' Jane said.

'What?'

'Don't know. I asked him once where they were and he said he had been asked to go and give a talk about the war to some school or other in Birmingham. I haven't a clue why they asked him – not exactly his thing, the war, was it? Anyway, he took the things and I gather some kid came up after the talk and asked lots of intelligent questions and Dad gave him Robbie's medals and things.'

'Oh! I ...'

'Just gave them away to a perfect stranger. Never asked if we might want them, did he? You know what Dad was like.'

After she had put the phone down Rachel thought about what her sister had said. After all, she had not wanted the medals specially. She had not thought of them for years and what would she do with a Gurkha knife? She had plenty of stuff of her own. They had been good at travelling light – Mum and Dad. Was that admirable or was it a disregard for family loyalties? Or both?

CHRIS

Date: 4 January 2015
Subject: Chris
Dear Jane,
Just home from London. Tried to ring but you're out. Just to say I am really concerned about Chris and have decided to go back down to stay with her as soon as I can fix things up here. Hope we can speak in the morning.
　　Love, R.

Text message: Sorry Hannah. Won't be able to make coffee on Wed. Going back to London. Will ring. Luv, R.

Rachel sat at her desk in her dressing gown nursing a cup of hot chocolate. The London train had been late and the queue for taxis had stretched round the corner of the station where the wind whipped through the Victorian facade. When she had eventually got in, the house felt dark and cold. She had made a hot drink and sat at the laptop to send some messages but now she felt suddenly she needed to rest. She needed to sleep. But most of all she needed to cry.

When Chris had rung just a couple of days before Christmas and said she couldn't come up to Manchester after all Rachel had thought it was just the usual Chris thing, saying she would come and then pulling out at the last moment, with some excuse which meant that she couldn't face it, meaning she couldn't face the family, or perhaps she couldn't face Rachel. It was hurtful but she had done it before and not only at Christmas. It was the old push-pull thing with Chris. Rachel, trying to keep the annoyance out of her voice, had said, 'Okay, well shall I come down in early January?' Then, when Chris phoned on New Year's Day and said, 'Rachel, can you come down soon? I am not feeling too good,' she had – of course – got on the first possible train and gone. She knew that Chris had not been feeling great. She had, Rachel remembered, cancelled a walking holiday she had planned for the late autumn because she wasn't feeling 'up to it'.

When Rachel phoned from Euston to say she was on her way, Chris told her to ring the doorbell for the basement flat and Jeff would let her in. Jeff was concerned. 'She's not been well. Glad you're here. Her door's on the latch.' Rachel climbed the narrow stairs. Those wretched buttons you had to push to keep the light on always went off before you got to the next landing, leaving you groping and stumbling on the spiral stairs. She pushed open the door of Chris's flat. The stench of cat shit made her want to retch. Chris sat, wearing her dressing gown, in her old arm chair. She was hunched over her stomach, her face that of an old woman, gaunt and drawn with pain.

'Sorry, I didn't come for Christmas but I am not too good,' Chris had said, smiling faintly. 'Chris!' Rachel went to put her arms round her. 'I had no idea …'

That was it. She had no idea. She was shocked to see how ill Chris looked. But Rachel had gone all brisk and efficient, made them both a cup of tea – without milk, as the dregs of the bottle in the fridge had gone off. Chris sipped the tea and then Rachel made her a hot-water bottle and persuaded her to go to bed. She shuffled into the bedroom bent over and lay down with a sigh. Rachel fed the cat, dealt with its tray and started to sort out the fridge, which meant more or less emptying it and cleaning it out.

Now back home, she felt the tears coming. She went to put the kettle on for a hot-water bottle and perhaps another hot drink but changed her mind and rummaged in the back of a cupboard for the single malt she had been given for Christmas. Instead of going to bed she took the hot toddy upstairs and opened the laptop again.

Date: 4 January 2005
Subject: Chris Again
Dear Both,
Just a follow-up to my last and my phone calls from London. As you know, Chris's phone is in her living room and it's impossible to have a private conversation in that flat. My mobile had run out of juice as I had forgotten to bring my charger. Didn't think I'd be at Chris's for more than 24 hours.

I am really concerned about her. She's very ill. Can hardly get out of her chair. We got an emergency appointment at the doc's and I went with her yesterday, drove her in the car and then sat in it while she went in but it was useless, I think. The Doc saw her for about three minutes and, as far as I can make out, said, 'You're a neurotic middle-aged woman. Go home and stop bothering me.' Didn't even examine Chris's stomach, which is hugely distended, and told her to take paracetamol. Wished I'd gone in and made a fuss but Chris is a grown up and I can't interfere. And she wouldn't let me, fair enough but she is really not up to it.

She has an out-patient appointment at the hospital for the 17th and she and I are trying to get that moved forward but hospital bureaucracy and aftermath of New Year seem to be making it impossible. Hours on the phone.

Obviously, Chris has not been able to look after herself properly for ages. The place stank – she must have got used to the smell – and the fridge was full of rotting food. I did a clear up and then a bit of a shop, made soup, which is about all she can eat but she didn't get much of that down. I think she was really pleased I was there and we talked a bit but she didn't have much energy. I was just going to stay for the one night but stayed the two in the end, as you know. Got back here late this pm and about to go to bed as I'm knackered. I've decided to sort stuff out here re work and things and go back down for a few days if I can. I really don't think Chris shd be on her own. I'll try to ring you both tomorrow.

Lotsaluv,

R

Date: 6 January 2005
Subject: Chris Again

Just to add to phone message. Chris left a message for me this pm that her hospital appointment's been moved forward. I'm going back down – hopefully tomorrow. One advantage of working part-time now is I can do that but I have various things I was committed to here and wanted to catch up with people and sort my house out after the Christmas chaos. Things not good with Chris, I fear, but we'll keep in touch,

R.

CHRIS

Rachel's Journal
6 January 2005

I woke early so am sitting up in bed writing this before getting up and packing my bag to go back down to London to be with Chris.

Last time she came up for Christmas must have been two years ago, no, it must have been three. I jumble the years up now in my memory. I had just invited her, no one else, and told her we'd have a quiet time. She didn't back down at the last minute. I met her at the station on Christmas Eve. I remember waiting in the station forecourt and seeing her come along looking great, I thought, with her bangles and her pretty shoes – something I never could manage. We had what I thought was quite a pleasant time together, going to church, opening a few presents – nothing over the top – a nice dinner, walk in the Park, just the three of us, Peter, Chris and me. Chris told me as we walked through the park that some bloke was wanting to marry her. She had told me various things needed sorting out but she obviously really fancied him. Her love life is a mystery to me. But walking in the park that Christmas Day she said she didn't feel it was too late to find someone she could spend her old age with.

Then on Boxing Day she suddenly said she had to get back home, she couldn't stand it anymore. She was clearly distressed, coming downstairs huddled up in an old dressing gown I'd lent her. I gave her a cup of tea and said, 'What's wrong, Chris?' but she wouldn't or couldn't say, just repeated that she had to get back home. When I said, 'But there aren't any trains on Boxing Day', she went back to bed and only got up so I could drive her to the station next morning.

It is such a pattern, the pull-push, of Chris's love. 'Come here – go away', mostly in our adult life I think, it's been the push, the 'go away'. But perhaps, perhaps, I feel now that it was not her, it was me who put the distance between us, it was my self-absorption, my not looking out for my little sister which opened the rift. All those years when we hardly spoke to each other, got news through Mum and Dad. I didn't have a clue how she was living – or even where sometimes. And after she left nursing and became a counsellor I did not really understand some of what she was into – or perhaps sympathise with it. I remember her telling me that everything about us was laid down in the first three months in the womb and I said, I thought quite mildly, that it seemed a bit biologistic or determinist or something and she got really angry with me.

Of course, the push-pull of her love was even more powerful with Mum and Dad. In so many ways, and not just in her consistent Christian faith, she was the one of us four who was closest to them, the one who went to be with them when they went back to India and were in Chennai and she stayed with them and worked for a few months in that village clinic (and caught TB). But, she has also been the one who has raged at them, blamed them for what they did to her – to us. That time I visited Mum and Dad in Birmingham not long before they moved to the Abbeyfield house in Herne Hill. Chris had just had a huge row with them and slammed out of the house and driven off in a rage. She had told Mum that all her (Chris's) problems were caused because Mum had rejected her in the womb. (This was the view of her latest therapist, which she had also told me about, he thought everything was laid down in the womb and, of course, was always the mother's fault.) Mum kept saying to me, 'But I was so happy in that pregnancy! I so much wanted that baby! I wanted you to have a little brother or sister.' Poor Mum! Poor Chris! Of course, then Mum said, 'If only Chris had got married and had children like the rest of you.' And went off into her usual riff. No wonder Chris felt sometimes that she didn't measure up.

But the last few years it was Dad Chris blamed for our childhood. I know once she said to me, 'Dad just doesn't get it. He doesn't get it.' I think she is still furious with him all these years after he has died.

Must get up and get sorted to go down to London. Really anxious about Chris. I did wonder whether she would just tell me to go back home but she's been really pleased that now I can be there. And I am glad, too.

8 January. PM.
Sitting up in bed in Chris's flat. It's early but she has gone to bed and I think she is asleep. I quite like this little room where she does her counselling, with its view across the London roofs towards the City and St Paul's. There are a few books on the shelf, mostly about therapy or psychoanalysis. Got down Juliet Mitchell's 'Mad Men and Medusas' but I wasn't quite up to reading about sibling relationships (enough of those going on in my life), so went back to my Margaret Atwood.

CHRIS

Chris is weaker if anything and really not eating at all. I am so glad the hospital appointment has been brought forward to tomorrow.

She and I got into a muddle today which nearly turned into a row about money. I had done some shopping and Chris was terribly anxious to repay me and got really upset when I said, 'It's OK. Pay me back later.' So in the end she told me her pin number and gave me her card so I could go and get money out of the hole in the wall, and she could pay me all of £6.42 or something. I remembered that time I came down a year or so ago and we went around Borough market, which Chris loves so much, and stopped for a coffee. Chris got really agitated at the counter, her hands were shaking and she couldn't get the money out of her purse, I said 'My treat' and she was obviously so relieved. I do realise she has a bit of a thing about money but still.

9 January
Woke very early. Daren't go and make a cup of tea for fear of disturbing cat. No sound from Chris. So glad she is going to the hospital today. She's so much worse, I am not sure she is going to be able to get downstairs – or more to the point – get back up those horrible stairs into the flat again. I nearly lost my footing and fell down a flight carrying out the rubbish bag to put in the bin yesterday It doesn't help to have those bloody light things you press which go off when you're half way down and leave you in the dark.

I have persuaded Chris to get a mini-cab to take us to St Thomas's. She really is not fit to drive and parking is a problem. I said I would organise and pay for the cab and we nearly got into a row about money again so I said, 'Let's not go there. You pay. That's fine.' We were sitting together in Chris's front room. I was drinking a cup of tea and she was sipping hot water. Then she said, 'You know, it's the obsessions, don't you?' I said, 'Yes, I do,' but of course I don't really, even though Chris did tell me last year about the diagnosis that her new therapist had come up with. O.C.D. she said it was, Obsessive Compulsive Disorder. She can't really talk to me about it, though we have tried. I know that this therapist, 'Ann', I think she's called, has told Chris that CBT (Cognitive Behaviour Therapy, all these bloody acronyms) does help with this condition sometimes.

We did talk about it a few months ago. Chris didn't think much of Cognitive whatsit– being into the talking cure, I suppose – but she had gone along for a diagnostic interview and come back really elated, as she felt that it might help her. She rang to tell me. Then she got a letter saying there was a year's waiting list for the treatment. It was that time I was down here briefly last spring, and Chris was devastated. Said it felt like she was drowning and someone had thrown her a life line only to snatch it away just as she grasped it. I think I had just begun to realise how much energy it took her to deal with her obsessions or whatever they are. We didn't talk about it yesterday. She really does seem to have very low energy. It's all she can do to get up and sit in a chair with the cat on her knee.

It's pretty, her room, very Chris somehow, with its plants and its pictures and knick-knacks but the old settees she's got with their flowery covers are not very comfortable, so I brought in the big chair from her therapy room where I am sleeping, for Chris to sit in.

No sound yet. I met one of Chris' neighbours yesterday evening coming in from the bins. She's the lady who lives on the ground floor and, according to Chris, has a thing about paper, collects paper bags, etc. They are a rather eccentric lot, as Chris says, but they all look out for each other and they all seem genuinely concerned about Chris. Jeff, the retired violinist, seems lovely and has been up from the basement to see if he can do anything.

I was trying to get Chris's ancient computer to work yesterday. In the end she rang Martin, the local vicar, who came bounding in yesterday afternoon. He was great, sat at the computer and managed to sort out at least some of the problems and then he sat and talked to Chris while I went out to the shops. Chris really likes him though she does not go to his church as she attends the Cathedral. He's quite camp and apparently, like most of the vicars in central London, is gay and lives with his partner. When he left he gave me his mobile number and told me to keep him in touch with how Chris was.

Time to get up and start to get ready for hospital visit. Feed old Narky. Etc.

9 January
Dear Jeff,
I am Chris's sister and we met a couple of days ago. Just to let you know that I went with Chris to the hospital this morning

and they are keeping her in and doing tests. She is very poorly but I think relieved that at last someone medical is taking her seriously. I wonder if you would mind looking after the cat for a few days. I am sorry to bother you but I am going to stay with my daughter in Archway. I think you must both be out or not answering the bell. Could you give me a ring on my mobile (0971234800) to let me know when you have picked up this note. I'll keep you in touch with what's going on.

Thanks,
Rachel

Date: 28 January 2005
Subject: Chris Again

Hi Sis. I know you're working away today and will be home late. I'm going to bed now and will go back to the hospital early so this is just to follow up our phone conversation and put you in the picture. I'm on Chris's ancient computer which keeps crashing, so hope this gets to you.

Am still trying to negotiate Chris's acceptance by the hospice at Clapham. She is very clear that is where she wants to go. They don't have a bed at the moment and I think it is a case of dead men's shoes, or rather dead women's beds. Awful! I still can't believe it. It has all been so quick. However, Chris is quite adamant that she wants no more chemo and the oncologists say she can't stand it and anyway it will only give her a short time more, even if it works. The cancer is so advanced.

Chris has also said she doesn't want any other intervention. Today she had a visitation from some frightfully top notch consultant. He swept in wearing a bow-tie with a train of attendant registrars after him. Chris and I have taken to calling the surgeons, 'sharks'. They swim through the hospital in shoals deciding who to cut up. The consultant oncologists are complete different. They treat you – or rather they treat Chris – like a human being.

Anyway, the top shark came in and said to me, 'Who are you?' When I said 'Chris's sister', he asked me to leave so that he could speak to her on her own. But Chris had asked me to stay as she finds him very intimidating. So I said; 'I'll go if my sister asks me to.' He huffed and puffed and said her family were obstructing her treatment and all the registrars looked at their shoes. I said, 'Chris, what do you want?' and she said, 'It's OK. you go. I'll cope!' So I went and waited outside the door.

It turned out he wanted to do an op to insert a tube into her stomach. She said she didn't want any more interventions. She knew she didn't have much time and she wanted to go to a hospice. After a while they all swept out again, glaring at me. I think she did amazingly. Apparently he is some very big cheese and this op is his pet project. Of course, Chris was completely exhausted by this and we both had a big cry and then she asked the nurse to help her get out of bed so she could sit in her chair by the window and we just sat and looked out at the river with the boats going up and down in front of the Houses of Parliament. I am so glad she has that room with its huge window and that she is there in the middle of south London by the river which she loves. We've always had a bit of a joke that whenever I come to visit her she says, 'Let's go and walk along the South Bank.' We sat for quite a long time without talking and watched the sky and river getting darker and the lights coming on along the bank and on the Big Ben tower.

The oncologist came in at the end of the afternoon and talked to Chris. Her view is that the procedure with the tube in the stomach isn't relevant to Chris's case, since she doesn't have a problem with swallowing but with keeping food down. She is getting thinner and thinner. Chris told the oncologist that she had trained in this same hospital – before the new building, of course, and they had a good conversation about how things have changed. They felt like two professionals talking as equals while I looked on.

This is the same oncologist who came in last week and sat on Chris's bed and said, 'Have you made your will?' and when Chris said 'No' told her she ought to. I was so shocked and angry at first but I think you were right. It galvanised Chris. She somehow – I don't know – she decided to do her own dying, or that dying was how she was going to live now. I think someone being honest with her was what she needed. So I shouldn't slag the hospital off because they have given Chris a lot. Having a room on her own, all on the NHS, has been wonderful. Still, I think what she wants now is to go to the hospice. I'll ring you tomorrow sometime.

Hope your training day went well,

Much love, R.

28 January

Dear Jeff,

Sorry to miss you again but Chris was very concerned that I gave you some money to pay for the cat food. So I am enclosing in this envelope the £20.00 she gave me. Can you let me know what else she owes you? I know you don't want to be paid but she is anxious to make sure you are not out of pocket.

It was lovely to see you yesterday at the hospital and I am sorry about the kerfuffle over letting you in. The trouble is that Chris has been getting so many visitors. At least that is the trouble from the Ward Sister's point of view. For Chris, of course, it is wonderful. However, she does get very exhausted, so the Sister ruled that only family could visit. Then all these different people kept turning up saying they had come all the way from Wales, etc., and Sister got rather cross. That's why we had that discussion when you arrived. I explained to her that really you were Chris's 'family', even though you were not related. So glad she let you in.

I'll let you know about the hospice.

Love to you both,

Rachel

Date: 3 February 2005

Subject: Chris Again

Dear J and J,

Just a quick note to follow up our various conversations. I've managed to negotiate only going into work one day a week so I can be down in London the rest of the week. Sleeping on K's sofa is not ideal but she says it is fine and the Northern Line (groan), goes direct from Archway so once I'm on the tube I can just sit there until I get to Clapham. As you saw when you were there, the hospice staff are wonderful and just accept that family and friends will want to be around. So I will go back down later today and stay for the rest of the week. Like you, I wish Chris had a room of her own but at least she is there in the hospice now and she is so much more comfortable than she was. The fact that the doctors discuss her treatment with her each day and allow her to say what she wants gives her back some control over what is going on. I know the choice between being so drugged up that you don't feel pain but are not really with it and having pain but being able to be more aware of what is going on is not a great choice!

Luv. R

Date: 6 February 2005
Subject: Chris
Dear J and J,
Hope you both got home safely. Chris was so pleased we were all able to be there together. She was exhausted, of course, so I came back to K's early last night. Had a longer day today but am back in K's flat now and using her computer. Just to keep you up to date. Chris is about the same. Doctor had a long talk with her this morning about the medication and how she can control it. I sat in the day room and had a good cry.

Jeff came to see her this afternoon and smuggled Sparky in in a cardboard box. I'm really not sure how he got away with it and I think the nurses just pretended they didn't know what was going on. There was no one else in the room except the woman in the corner who is unconscious now, and her daughter who was sitting with her. Jeff opened the box and the cat shot under the bed. I tried to coax him out but you know what a bad-tempered animal it is, so I got well scratched. In the end Jeff managed to get Sparky to sit on the bed where he settled down, purring away. Chris was delighted. Jeff couldn't stop long and we had a struggle to get the cat back into the box but it was worth it.

So many people want to come and visit her that I have said I am appointing myself Chris's social secretary. It is humbling – all those people who love her and were with her for all those years when I hardly saw her. There are a lot of them! The Hospice Office said they were going to have to appoint an extra member of staff to deal with all the post and phone calls she is generating. Joking apart, it is complicated as of course she wants to see everyone who comes, she wants to say goodbye to her friends, but she gets worn out. I sometimes feel like telling people to go away, especially when they seem to want Chris to make it all OK with them that she is dying. One woman in particular completely wore her out.

I think it was the day before yesterday but I lose track. Anyway, I had taken Chris in the wheelchair into the day room so she could have time with her friend and I went for a walk in the garden but when I came back, at the time we'd agreed, this woman wouldn't go but kept crying and holding on to Chris's hand. In the end Chris just said 'Ive got to go now' and I wheeled her back and asked the nurse to help her back into bed, where she lay with her eyes closed. I felt so angry with the woman that I had to put my coat back on and go and stamp about in the garden for a bit. I realised I was furious with everyone, including Chris for dying.

Jim, it was great to see you and, Jane, let me know when you will be able to come down to London and don't feel bad. I know you can't be here as much as I can. I just feel glad that I can though, of course – well, you know.

I'll have my mobile. Lots of love,

R.

69, St Anselm's Rd
Manchester
14 April 2005
Dear Anne Morrow,

Forgive me writing to you out of the blue like this. I am Chris's sister and I found your address in her address book which I have been going through while dealing with her affairs and clearing her flat after her death. I think you were at her funeral last month but there were such a lot of people there (I've only come to realise these last few weeks how many people felt connected to and loved my sister). Her friend, Jennifer, said you had slipped away at the end of the service, so we didn't meet.

It was a wonderful occasion, wasn't it? Of course, so much of it was what she planned in those last few days– Jeff playing his violin, the Peruvian Alleluia and the rest of the music. I think she would have liked the willow coffin, too. You know how courageous she was. She was sustained by her faith, of course, but also, I think by having faced up to some very hard things during her life, so when death came, she had had a lot of practice. Still, she had some moments of dread about going into the dark and one evening in the hospice she told me that she knew it was stupid but she couldn't bear the idea of the coffin being closed over her. I said I'd make sure it didn't happen. But, then the undertakers said coffins had to have lids on them. So, the woven willow coffin seemed right.

I am writing because I would very much like to come and see you if I may and also because I want to ask your advice as Chris's therapist. Towards the end of her time in the hospice (brief enough) while she could still speak Chris told me that for years she had been keeping a journal, mostly trying to plot the progress of her OCD, though it was only recently and thanks to your support that she was able to give it a name. I feel so sad that it was only in these last couple of years that Chris could talk to me about the OCD and I began to realise something of what she had battled with for her whole life. It made sense of such a lot of things which had always been upsetting about her behaviour. Like the way she would suddenly say she had to go home when you thought she had come for a few days' visit.

One of the worst things about going through her post was finding the appointment for the course of Cognitive Behaviour Therapy which, I think, you encouraged her to try. The letter came while she was in the hospice. I didn't tell her. Her first appointment was for three days before the day she died. I don't know if it would have helped but I am upset that she never had a chance to try it.

So, about the notebooks-journal, Chris told me about them when she had been in the hospice for about a week. As you know it was all so quick and she was trying to sort things out as she could. (We had written her will the day before, in the ward with a visitor from the room across the way as a witness. Turned out he was some rather shady South London character but she didn't exactly have a fortune and the bit of paper we wrote on was accepted as her will.) She told me where the notebooks were and asked me to destroy them and I said I would. Then a few days later, when she was much further down and barely able to speak, she said – and it was a huge effort – 'Those notebooks. If there is anything there which might help someone, you could keep them.' I said. 'All right.' I tried to help her get comfortable but she so much wanted to say something and it was so hard for her. I couldn't quite catch but I think it was 'Ask Ann', which is why I am asking you now. I have found a whole pile of her notebook-journals. I have to confess I did start reading one of them, partly because it was in with a lot of other papers I was going through. Then I thought, 'I think this is not something I should read'. My own strong feeling now is that I should destroy them but I wanted to know what you thought was right and what it might mean for someone to 'find them helpful'.

Could you ring me or write to me at the address on the top of this letter. We, my brother and sister and I, have nearly cleared Chris's flat and we are putting it on the market this week but I will still be up and down to London regularly so could meet you whenever is convenient to you, if you felt OK about that.

Many thanks,
Rachel

25 May 2005
Dear Anne,
Thanks for meeting me. It was very helpful. I feel very upset that I never realised what it meant for Chris to battle all her life with these obsessions and I blame myself for not being able to speak about it until the very end of her life. I don't think any of us – her family – realised how ill she was. She tried to hide it and I don't think I really gave her proper attention through most of our adult life – only at the very end when she was dying. You know because I was older than her by eighteen months I was always told I had to look after her, my little sister. Somehow, I think those struggles she had with despair and obsession meant she befriended a lot of people – all those people who came to see her in the hospice and came to her funeral. And, of course, she could also be great fun!

I have decided to destroy all her notebooks. I have, however, kept some of her art work. She had done some wonderful chalk sketches and a couple of paintings of a convent place in Wales she loved. I am getting those framed.

Thank you again,
Rachel

X
LAST THINGS
(2005/2016)

'... AND ASHES'

'**S**weet Thames runs softly till I end my song.'
That was the problem, Rachel thought, of being so literary. Everything came filtered through quotation. But the river *was* sweet this morning, if you could use the word now without post-modern irony. It smelled of itself and faintly of the sea as the tide swirled up past the moored house-boats and barges. Rachel leaned against the side of the boat as the engine began to chug, taking them out into the main stream. It was a blue May morning, a lover's morning, hey ding-a-ding-a-ding. The water glinted and dazzled. Rachel looked down into the darkness under the boat, which now began to move, slow and stately, into the main stream. They said salmon might return to the Thames again now that all those centuries of pollution and rubbish were being cleared. Dust and ashes. The mud banks, which were now disappearing under the rising tide, had been scavenged throughout the nineteenth century by men, women and children looking for any bits of rubbish that might be of value. 'Mudlarks', Henry Mayhew had called them in his account of the London of the 1850s. They must have been like the rag-pickers in modern day Indian cities, the children scrabbling on the rubbish dumps.

The docks had gone; there was a block of expensive high rise flats behind the mooring place. Jim had been telling her how the city bankers who had moved into the new development had objected to the huddle of barges and house boats moored below them because they 'spoiled the view'. Rachel couldn't understand how anyone could object to the painted boats with their boxes of bright flowers. The barge they were on was beautiful, its exterior painted in elaborate flowered patterns, the inside all polished wood and elegantly managed living space. There was even a piano for heaven's sake.

'It belongs to some friends,' was all Jim would say, 'and I

229

explained what we wanted and they are happy to take us out for the morning.' The bearded man at the back holding the wooden tiller nodded and smiled at Rachel as they began to move upstream, towards Westminster.

They were all there, the family, mostly standing and looking at the river. The passing buildings glittered in the morning sunshine. 'Earth hath not anything to show more fair', Rachel thought. No wonder Chrissie loved it so much. Jane came and put an arm round her.

'I was just thinking of how every time I came to London, Chris would say, "let's go and see the river" and we'd come down and walk along the South Bank,' Rachel said,

'She did love it,' Jane nodded. There were tears in her eyes.

'But I don't think I've seen it from here before.'

'Didn't you ever get one of those tourist boats from Westminster to Greenwich?' said Jane.

'Oh Yes. Perhaps. Years ago. It looks very different now.'

Their brother came and joined them, leaning against the side of the boat. 'I was remembering when we went up to Northumberland to scatter Mum and Dad's ashes,' he said. 'That was another lovely spring day.' They were all silent for a moment thinking of the moors above their grandmother's house. 'At least we don't have to lug the ashes up a hill today,' said James. 'Ashes are surprisingly heavy.'

'Have you got them?'

'Yes, picked them up yesterday. I think we should wait until we get well upstream, past Westminster and St Thomas's. Perhaps we shouldn't do it immediately opposite the Houses of Parliament. It's illegal to scatter ashes on the Thames, you know.'

'Who said?'

'I consulted one of my friends who knows about these things.' Jim had knowledgeable friends in high and low places all over London. 'Then I rang the Council and they said it was absolutely forbidden. However, if you are a Sikh you can get special dispensation. So we are being Sikhs today.'

They were passing under Blackfriars Bridge.

'Well, Chris was very clear about what she wanted. So if we get arrested by the River Police or whatever …' A steamer went past full of tourists who waved. They waved back. Jane's husband, William, was pointing out landmarks to Rachel's daughters.

'Where are they?' Rachel asked Jim. He brought out a plastic bag in which she saw a brown plastic jar, a bit like a large kitchen jar. She took off the lid and looked inside at the grey-white mixture. Her mind would not connect.

The boat was passing the Palace of Westminster, which flaunted its pinnacles at the windows of St Thomas's Hospital opposite. Rachel looked up and tried to identify the window which had been Chris's that last time. Then the boat was turning and beginning to drift down stream. The glug, glug of water slapping under the bow turned to a softer sound. The noise of traffic came from the Embankment.

'Here?'

'I think so.'

Dust and ashes.

But ash is wayward and does not fall neatly. It flies in the wind or sticks to the tires on the side of the boat.

But it is not her. For she is not here.

Sweet Thames run softly till I end my song.

THE TROUBLE WITH THINGS

It wasn't just old letters. It was things! She just had too many of them. Rachel surveyed the comfortable clutter of her bedroom. It was Saturday and, obedient to the rhythms of many years, she was cleaning the house. Of course, now she was retired she was not bound to work timetables. She did not have to get up and go out of the house every weekday morning with a head full of 'must-dos'. She could clean the house any time of day or night. Or not clean it at all, she thought, looking at the layer of dust on the book case. Yes, as her younger friends in work pointed out to her enviously, now she could do what she liked when she liked. But such freedom took practice. It was the same with living on your own. It was like learning to ride a bicycle in old age, balancing on ridiculously thin surfaces. She had got used to having stabilisers. Rachel remembered once in the basement of the old Frontline Books, long gone the way of all small, radical bookshops, she had heard the novelist Buchi Emecheta speaking about the moment when her last child left home. Going into the supermarket, she had said to herself, 'Now I can buy what *I* want to eat' - but then, wandering round with her basket, she found she did not know anymore what it was she wanted.

Some days Rachel felt the spaciousness of her new life. The silence and solitude of the house held her. When she woke she would carry a cup of tea upstairs and have what she called her 'quiet time', the time she chose to be quiet. That was the secret. To choose the silence. Not to put the radio on. Not to text her daughter or her friend. To practise the scales and arpeggios of silence as she had practised her music those many hours in the monkish cells at school. To be. Just to be in the present and accept the silence.

Sometimes, she found it hard. Clutter, that was the problem.

THE TROUBLE WITH THINGS

All the clutter. In her head and in the room. She looked around at the pile of books and yesterday's newspaper lying by the bed. On the chest of drawers was a lop-sided gondola bought fifteen years ago by her godson with his very own money; the soft sculpture hamburger from a daughter's long ago art lesson; the detritus of a lifetime. She started to dust the photos of her family which stood on the low book case, starting with the photos of her grandchildren which she had printed off from the email. But alongside them were the old ones, Mum and Dad on their sixtieth wedding anniversary, surrounded by the family, in the garden of the Abbeyfield House in Herne Hill wearing the garlands supplied by Mohan, their old friend from Chennai (or could we say Madras?).

Where should she start? She looked at the top of the chest of drawers near the bed. Such unfashionable old furniture, bought in an auction when she and Peter had first got married and now despised as 'brown stuff'. She had seen one just like it in the warehouse of the local charity which provided housing for destitute asylum seekers. Should she start with the old sewing box, perhaps. Granny had called it her 'work box'. Its dark wood, inlaid with mother of pearl, gleamed a little. Granny herself had inherited it from some now forgotten relative. 'Her Aunt Christina, your great-great aunt,' Auntie Nan had said, and she in turn had been given it by another relative who had bought it at the Great Exhibition of 1851 – or so Nan had said and she had been the family historian. Rachel would never have thought of addressing Nancy just like that without the honorific 'Auntie'. Auntie Nancy, and all the other aunties, they stretched out beyond the walls of her bedroom, the familiar dead, back and back. What was it the Bible said? 'Seeing we are surrounded by so great a cloud of witnesses.' Sometime, fancifully, she imagined them as in a theatre, stacked up tier on tier, looking down at the brightly lit stage of the present.

The workbox stood, square and solid, a symbol of the relative wealth of her father's family. Her mother's Irish ancestors had left no such substantial traces. Rachel stroked the dark wood, lifted the lid. Inside, the red satin lining was worn and gaped here and there. There were old spools for cotton with mother-of pearl tops and ancient reels of high-quality thread now jumbled up with old packets of needles, various buttons, a frayed tape measure which folded away into a little box decorated with a blue flower. Rachel lifted out the top drawer and rummaged about in the bottom. Among the old knitting needles, she found a darning mushroom. How many years was it since she had darned a sock? Yet, she had been a good darner, and there had been something satisfying about that weaving in and out, catching up the threads, making good again. Rachel suddenly remembered her grandmother sitting by the fire and knitting socks, her arthritic fingers moving slowly through the wool. It was such an unlikely memory she wondered if she had made it up. Granny was no domestic goddess. Nor was she a cosy granny with a knee. She did knit, however, and somewhere in the box Rachel thought, were old knitting needles. She rummaged again and found a recent addition, a spool of transparent tape, the kind you could use to iron into your trouser hem when the stitching gave way. 'You're not still sewing trouser hems, are you?' her friend Jenny had said to her. 'I'll get you some of that iron-on tape. One of the wonders of modern technology.'

How great, Rachel thought, that for my generation of women, 'work' did not simply equate with sewing. Even relatively privileged women like her father's mother had been caught in that trap. My generation! Rachel thought, those much despised feminists of the '70s, but perhaps we helped to make a world where a woman's worth was no longer measured by the neatness of her stitches. 'She would work better if she talked less', Miss D. had said on one of her school reports and there was that blue and white gingham apron, which became grubbier and grubbier with unpicked and re-sewn stitches and bloody traces in the cotton which she had spent her first year at school making. Auntie May had not been much impressed with it. But then, Rachel had never been good at making her stitches invisible.

That was it! Darning, sewing, cleaning, all that labour which held the fabric of ordinary life together, women's work, it all had to be made invisible. Still was – even though darning was no longer taught in schools. She could darn but how she had fretted at the hours spent in mindless repetitive work, darns holding darns together. She had only slowly realised that what she was being taught was not just mending. They were practising for a life of invisible labour: cleaning, dusting, scrubbing down walls and floors, cooking, wiping bottoms, and, of course, patching up quarrels, weaving words across gaps. Women's work. The crucial work of holding things together.

She'd joined the Women's Liberation Movement, written about making invisible women visible and still she had spent more hours of life on domestic labour than she wanted to remember. How deeply engrained it was! Here she was cleaning the house on a Saturday, as she had done throughout her years of paid work, playing jazz loudly on the radio as she had in the past. 'Get a cleaner,' her friends said. But she couldn't. She couldn't pass that work on to another woman. 'I must clean up my own mess,' she said to herself. She remembered the sweeper, the untouchable, the Dalit, woman, standing back on the stairs with her eyes cast down and her sari pulled over her head as the little white girl came past. I am that little girl, Rachel thought. I am not that little girl.

No. She could not get rid of the work box. She would keep it for her daughters. They could junk it or sell it after she was dead, or keep it perhaps – even, who knows, there might be a reaction against minimalism in furnishings and they might want to put it where they could see it, touch it. Or mending and making do might come back into fashion.

On the other side of the chest of drawers was an Indian basket. She could not remember exactly where it came from but it was part of the debris not just of her Indian childhood, but of that high tide of colonialism whose receding had marked her early life. It was an example of those worked objects, (baskets, copperware, needlework) which she thought of as 'missionary work' and had for most of her life secretly despised. They were, she thought, the product of well-meaning missionaries setting up industrial schools or small workshops for fallen women or street children. The objects they produced were, Rachel had felt, rarely useful, though you could find them now in every Oxfam shop. They were produced for western markets using India's traditional skills in ways which never seemed to her to meet either the traditional or the new demands. Indians anyway didn't want traditionally crafted baskets or earthenware pots. They wanted plastic – hence the trail of plastic cups alongside every Indian railway where passengers had thrown them out of the carriage window, a habit which was fine when the cups sold on railway stations were traditional earthen-ware pots which disintegrated. It was not so good with plastic which would lie there for however many hundred years it takes to deteriorate. However, that might be changing. Her friend Katharine told her that plastic cups were no longer sold at Indian stations so maybe she was wrong about that.

Rachel had always had a particular horror for what she privately called 'missionary bags'. These were shoulder bags always woven in bright stripes, used –she had thought as a child – only by certain kinds of missionary lady. She would not be seen dead with one of these over her shoulder but when she turned out her sister's flat after her death, she had tired of sorting and throwing out and had in the end stuffed several black bin liners to take home and sort at leisure. So, she had found herself the owner of just such a bag.

'Oh, can I have this bag if you don't want it, Mum?' Her daughter was going through a load set aside for the Oxfam shop.

'Yes, love, if you really want it.'

'I think it's great. And I'm trying not to use plastic bags, so this will be useful – and I like it. It reminds me of Auntie Chris. Thanks.'

I was in the wrong, Rachel thought, wrong to be so contemptuous. Wrong to dismiss the missionary bag. It did, after all, have its own beauty and it cared for the earth as plastic did not.

Unlike the missionary bag, she had always liked the round basket which now sat among the ear-rings and half-empty jars of face cream on her chest of drawers. She had no idea what the basket was originally for. It looked like a smaller version of the snake charmer's basket, the one in which the snake lay curled up waiting for the lid to be lifted and the music of the pipe to rouse it into a swaying, dangerous dance. Whatever it had been intended for, she now used it as a medicine chest. The lid wouldn't quite fit over the assorted packets of paracetamol, strepsils sticky with age, a yellowing bandage. The colour of the basketry had faded to a uniform ivory. No. She could not get rid of this either. But she could get rid of some of the odd ear-rings and other bits of cheap jewellery, some of it presents from long ago, which she had never worn.

The bangles were her sister's and so, too the silver bracelet which Rachel had found on the dressing table when they were sorting through all Chris's things after she died. Chris was always the one who wore bracelets and bangles. How they had loved those thin, glass bangles as children! Mum had disapproved and said they were really for grownups. How they sparkled and tinkled on the wrists of the Indian women who wore rows of them to match the glowing colours of their saris! Rachel and Chris both resolved when they were grown up they would have heaps of bangles and Chris had gone on wearing them all her life. They were part of her style, her femininity. Rachel had never been a bangle-wearer but when she saw the silver bracelet among Chris's things she had wanted it. She wore it now from time to time in honour of her dead sister.

It had felt so intrusive going through Chris's private things after her death, the papers stuffed into her desk, the little mementos from holidays, her own and her friends', which cluttered the shelf above the gas fire. Rachel thought again of how Chris had gone for that outpatient's appointment at the hospital and been sent home 'just to pick up a sponge bag and night clothes' and then had never come back – never been able to say goodbye to her plants and ornaments and to her cat. She loved that flat.

They had discussed it with one of the nurses in the hospice, she and Jane and Jim.

'We can get a wheelchair for you,' the nurses had said.

'Yes. But the flat is up three flights of stairs.'

'Isn't there a lift?'

'No. It's a Georgian house, you know one of those old London squares – only all the other sides of the square were bombed and it's all council flats round it now. It's Saaf London, you know. Not posh.'

'I could carry her if someone helped me,' said James. 'She doesn't weigh much now.'

'James. Those stairs are only wide enough for one and they're really steep and windy ... You can't get two people side by side – let alone two people carrying a third.'

'I could carry her by myself in a fireman's lift,' he said. The nurse looked at him and they thought about Chris lying in bed with her pale face, her morphine drip in her arm. James's eyes filled with tears. 'She so wanted to,' he said.

Mum and Dad were good at travelling light, she thought. 'Ruthless,' Jane had said, 'giving away precious family things without asking any of us if we wanted them.' Perhaps you had to be ruthless. Death, after all, was pretty uncompromising. If she could start getting rid of some of these things, perhaps she could move lightly towards death. Freewheel into the unknown. Her first boyfriend had had a motor bike and she wasn't quite sure now whether she had loved him or loved that feeling of danger and excitement, riding on the pillion at an astonishing fifty miles an hour with the wind on your face and hair – no helmets then, of course. No motorways where bad boys could 'do the ton'.

Wasn't it better, then, to practise giving things up now? 'Goods and chattels' her father had called them – these small domestic objects. But were they goods? Dad and Mum didn't seem to think so and Christianity was, Rachel thought, at best ambivalent. Were they perhaps 'bads' rather than 'goods', the baskets and bangles and bits of pottery? If they were goods perhaps the thing to do was to hold on to them, cherish them, honour the histories made material in them. There was something called Thing Theory, which she gathered was all about this.

She picked up the mug in which she had drunk her early morning cup of tea. It was a blue Dartington mug which her daughter had given her last Christmas. Yes, she thought, such things embody relationships and memories but also the silent histories of their making and their care, the domestic labour which kept them clean and whole. They go on after their owners have gone – or at least some of them do. It depended on how well off you were, of course. She thought of the bare mud floors of the one-roomed Indian huts she had known in her childhood, houses where the few possessions were fragile and would not last beyond their owner's short lives – thin sleeping mats, earthenware cooking pots, the family clothes in a basket.

Chris's Indian bangles gleamed in the light falling from the window onto the chest of drawers.

AN ANGLO-INDIAN GLOSSARY

(According to Rachel with help from Yule and Burnell's *Hobson Jobson* Dictionary)

Almyra: a wardrobe

Bandy or Vundy: any kind of vehicle, a cart, a car.

Betel: a leaf chewed with a nut which produces a narcotic effect and a red staining juice.

Baksheesh: a tip or more often something given to a beggar; it is what all beggars say as they thrust their hands towards you; Yule and Burnell say there is no equivalent in English.

Budmash: Y and B. give 'one following evil courses', which sums it up pretty well.

Bund: a dam, embankment.

Bungalow: originally applied to the one-storey thatched house usually occupied by Europeans in India. It was taken up in general usage in Britain for one-storey houses but in twentieth century India was used of any colonial-type house regardless of roofing or whether it had one or two storeys.

Chitty, Chit: a note.

Chupples: flip-flops.

Collector: The title of the senior administrator of a District under, first, the East India Company and, then, the Raj. The name comes obviously from his primary role of collecting taxes.

Compound: the area around a colonial house or houses.

Congee: literally the water rice has been cooked in but generally used for any kind of grain-based sloppy food.

Dhobi: the man who washed clothes, traditionally by banging the wet clothes on a rock and leaving to dry in the sun; transferred sometimes to mean clothes needing washing.

Dhoty, dhoti: the strip of cloth worn by men. It is wrapped around the waist and then either worn hanging loose like a skirt or the end is caught between the legs and tucked into the waist. For any kind of physical work the latter method is preferred.

Ghat: the path up a mountain or through a pass; a mountain range.

Go-down: originally meaning a brick storehouse, came to be applied to any brick building; south Indian houses were traditionally built of mud, as many still are.

Gopuram: the tower over the entrance to a South Indian temple.

Hobson Jobson: originally a term for words from another language naturalised into native pronunciation, it has become associated with Yule and Burnell's *Dictionary, A Glossary of Colloquial Anglo-Indian Words and Phrases*.

Jutka: a covered ox-cart.

Kitchery, Kedgeree: rice and dahl cooked together and sometimes served at Anglo–Indian breakfast. It does not contain fish. Comes to mean a mixture, or perhaps a mixed jargon, like Anglo-Indian indeed!

Pucka: substantial, permanent, hence more generally 'proper', as contrasted with 'cutcha'.

Puja: prayers, worship.

Punchayet: village council, traditionally of five men.

Punkah: a large fan pulled by means of a rope which passes through a hole in the wall to an outside veranda or space where the 'punk-wallah' sits.

Ragi or raggy: a red grain grown as a staple in Southern India.

Shola: Hobson Jobson gives 'wooded ravine' and 'thicket' but it was a word generally used for any wood or clump of trees.

Tambi or thumbi: I had always understood it to mean something like 'little boy', 'little brother' – hence the joke of Big Tambi. Y and B do not give it at all but serendipitously I discovered, rooting about in their Glossary, that there is such a word used in Indonesia to mean something like 'peon' (pronounced pewn), the general Anglo-Indian word for 'messenger', which originally meant foot soldier.

Tank: an artificial pond, lake or receptacle in which water is collected. A bathing pool attached to a temple for ritual bathing.

Tatty: a screen or mat made of grasses or thin twigs loosely threaded together and hung in doors and other openings to keep out the sun. Hobson-Jobson specifies that these are damped to make the air cooler but I have no memory of this.

Topee: meant 'hat' but came to be used for the pith helmet traditionally worn by British Colonial men and their families, hence 'topee-wallers'. We never wore them.

Untouchables: now preferring, and generally receiving, the name 'Dalits'.

Veranda: colonial houses had roofed in galleries all round them to provide shade and keep the interior cool.

Wallah: a suffix affixed to a range of qualities or jobs and meaning, 'man', 'someone who does', but Hobson-Jobson provide a long and complex set of associations for it, mainly slightly derogatory – as befits the colonial power's view of those they governed.